The Restored Railways
of Yorkshire and Lancashire

The Restored Railways of Yorkshire and Lancashire

ANDREW WILSON

TEMPUS

To Chris for her patience and to all the volunteers who keep these railways operating.

First published 2006

Tempus Publishing Limited
The Mill, Brimscombe Port,
Stroud, Gloucestershire, GL5 2QG
www.tempus-publishing.com

British Library Cataloguing in Publication Data.
A catalogue record for this book is available from the British Library.

ISBN 0 7524 4132 9
978 0 7524 4132 0

Typesetting and origination by Tempus Publishing Limited.
Printed in Great Britain.

Contents

	Acknowledgements	6
	Introduction	7
one	The Middleton Railway	9
two	The Keighley & Worth Valley Railway	17
three	The North York Moors Railway	39
four	The National Railway Museum	57
five	The Embsay & Bolton Abbey Steam Railway	63
six	The Kirklees Light Railway	77
seven	The Wensleydale Railway	83
eight	Steamtown Carnforth	93
nine	The East Lancashire Railway	101
ten	The West Lancashire Light Railway	115
eleven	The Ribble Steam Railway	117
twelve	Dinting Railway Centre	123
thirteen	Other Railways and Steam Centres	127

Acknowledgements

I would like to thank all those people who have helped me with photographs: Michael Mensing, Audie Baker at the Kidderminster Railway Museum, the Lens of Sutton Association, Roger Carpenter and Richard Casserley. All the uncredited photographs were taken by me and any errors are mine and mine alone.

Introduction

Mention Yorkshire and Lancashire and images of the Wars of the Roses, the red rose against the white, immediately spring to mind. Cricket aficionados relish the matches at either Old Trafford or Headingley against the 'old enemy'. Association football matches where Leeds United are pitted against Manchester United, Sheffield Wednesday against Preston North End, are steeped in Lancashire versus Yorkshire rivalry. Rugby – both union and league – is the same, and yet the principal railway company to serve both of these northern counties was the Lancashire & Yorkshire Railway.

The history of the railways of these two counties is both complex and interesting. In Yorkshire a plethora of companies vied with each other for the traffic on offer, particularly the lucrative coal business, and as a consequence there was considerable duplication of lines and services. The same happened in Lancashire and so in the harsh economic environment of the late 1950s and early 1960s there were many lines whose existence could be challenged on the grounds that income was not covering expenses. Consequently when Dr Richard Beeching published his report 'The Reshaping of British Railways' and declared that the railways had lost £135.9m in 1961 the door to the closure of many supposedly unremunerative lines was flung open. Many of the lines that were eventually closed in Yorkshire and Lancashire may have lost money on paper but provided an important social service. The key phrase in the Beeching Report, as far as many lines were concerned, was the 'inability of the services to produce revenue sufficient to cover the direct costs of operating them'.

Among the lines to be closed after the Beeching Report were the Keighley to Oxenhope branch in West Yorkshire, the line between Malton, Pickering and Grosmont in North Yorkshire, the Ilkley to Skipton mainline via Bolton Abbey and Embsay and the Clayton West branch line, also in West Yorkshire. One North Yorkshire line between Northallerton and Hawes, however, had closed almost a decade before in 1954. To the west across the Pennines the same happened to the Bury to Rawtenstall line which succumbed in 1972.

Today these five lines are thriving thanks to the determination of groups of volunteer enthusiasts who refused to allow the lines to die. Money was raised, rolling stock was bought, rails and sleepers were replaced, leases were arranged and eventually services restarted. Looking at what some of these groups have achieved against all the odds one can only marvel at their foresight and sheer doggedness. Some of these 'preserved' railways have been operating for twice as long as under the auspices of British Railways.

Under the umbrella term of 'preserved railways' in Yorkshire and Lancashire are three lines that do not follow the pattern of post-Beeching closure. These are the Middleton Railway in Leeds, the West Lancashire Light Railway near Hesketh Bank and the Preston Dock Railway which owe their existence to different sets of circumstances. Again the central theme to their continued survival is the determination of sets of volunteers to enjoy their hobby and provide entertainment and education for the public in general.

The first of these railways that I came to know well was the Keighley and Worth Valley Railway. I was invited to the Bingley College of Education for an interview in March 1968 with a view to taking up a place on a teacher training course. After travelling from King's Cross to Leeds on a Deltic-hauled express I was ill-prepared for the drop in temperature as I waited for the connecting diesel multiple unit to take me along the Aire Valley to Bingley. The walk up Park Road and Lady Lane to the college was another shock to the system as a blizzard was blowing. The only thing I remember about the interview was talking to the two admissions tutors about railways and the soon to be opened steam railway based at nearby Haworth. Of course the rest is history, I was offered and accepted a place and as a result was a regular visitor to the Keighley and Worth Valley Railway.

When I qualified in 1972 my first teaching post was in the Bradford area. Having stayed in the area ever since I was able to discover the Middleton Railway and watch with interest the opening of the North York Moors Railway, the Embsay Steam Railway, the East Lancashire Railway, the Kirklees Light Railway, the Wensleydale Railway, the West Lancashire Light Railway and the Preston Docks Railway. It is these very different and varied railways that this book is about and the intervening four decades that have seen many of them mature and develop into some of the most important tourist destinations in England.

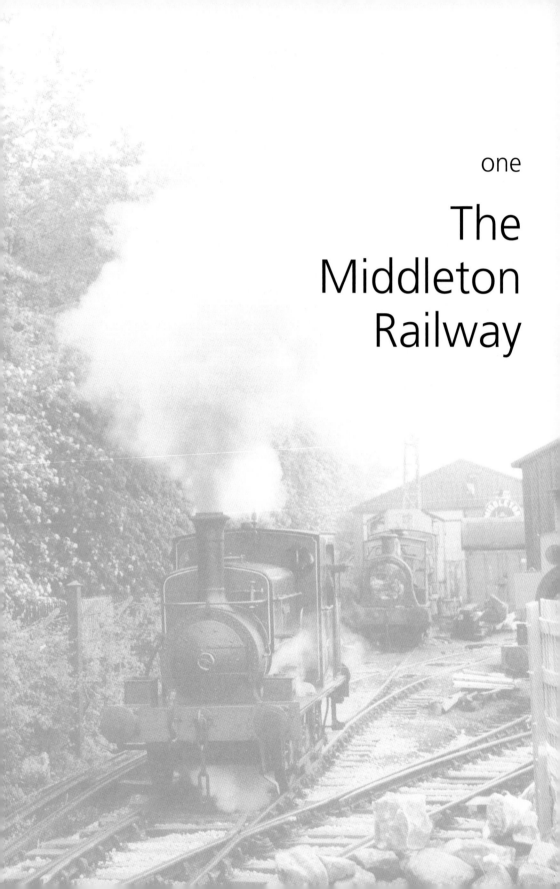

one

The
Middleton
Railway

The Middleton Railway at Hunslet, south of Leeds, can claim an impressive number of 'firsts' in the world of steam railways. It was the first railway to be authorised by Act of Parliament, the first to use steam locomotives and the first standard-gauge line to be successfully re-opened by enthusiasts. Another significant 'first' is that it still runs over much of its original route.

The Middleton Railway owes its existence to the coal deposits that lay beneath the open fields of Middleton, to the south of Leeds. In 1646 it is recorded that Sir Ferdinande Leigh was the owner of a 'cole myne' at Middleton. In 1717 Ralph Brandling was the owner of a 'wrought colliery or coal mine with a water engine and smithy' at Middleton. In 1755 Brandling obtained powers to construct a 960ft-long wooden waggonway on Woodhouse Hill Lane to get better access to the River Aire. Such was the output that on 9 June 1758 Brandling obtained a private Act of Parliament, the first for the construction of a railway or waggonway, to supply coal to Leeds, which in 1801 was the eighth largest town in Britain with a population of 53,000. By 1808 there were no less than 4 miles of waggonways, the precursor of the Middleton Railway.

The need to counter the increasing cost of horses and fodder, owing to the demands of the Napoleonic Wars, saw a local man, John Blenkinsop, invent a rack rail method of traction. When this was allied to Mathew Murray's first steam locomotive a solution to the escalating cost of using horses had been found. Murray's locomotive was capable of doing the work of thirteen horses and could pull twenty-seven waggons on the level at 3mph. The first two locomotives went into service on 12 August 1812. Unfortunately one of the locomotives blew up in 1818, killing the driver and scalding a number of children, but this accident did not slow progress. By 1827 an inclined line had been built from Belle Isle to Middleton village and by 1832 there was a rail link between Fanny Pit, New Lane and the top of the incline. Eight years later the line had been extended to West Pit.

In 1862 the Brandling Estates were sold to Tetley & Co. who formed the Middleton Estate & Colliery Co. The 4ft 1in lines were extended and two 0-4-0ST steam locomotives were built for the line by Manning & Wardle: *Blenkinsop* in 1866 and *Matthew Murray* in 1869. Further progress occurred in 1881 when the gauge of the lines was changed to 4ft 8in, standard gauge. The colliery lines continued to flourish and a link with the Midland Railway was completed in 1895. Four years later the Great Northern Railway opened a connection with the Middleton Colliery line near New Pit. Coal continued as the major traffic for many years but was joined by steel and scrap metal as new traders moved in to the area.

The development of the railway reflected the industrial development of this part of south Leeds ebbing and flowing in response to the concerns it served. Little now remains of the track and sidings around Broom Pit and New Pit, nor of that around the Coke Ovens, brickworks, clay pits and quarries. There were also three commercial sidings on Hunslet Moor that served Wagon Repairs Ltd, Clayton Son & Co., and Robinson & Birdsell, Metal Merchants, and John King & Co., Ironfounders. Eventually traffic north of Whitaker's Staiths ceased on 13 September 1948.

When the coal mines were nationalised the line came under the umbrella of the National Coal Board and for a time the Middleton Railway was used by the Hunslet locomotive firm of John Fowler to test its locomotives. The southern part of the line was cut back as coal workings were worked out and within a decade most of the line, except that from Parkside Great Northern Junction and Middleton Broom Pit, had been closed by the National Coal Board. As the fortunes of this part of Leeds went into decline the need to renew much of the track became essential and competition from road transport made this uneconomic, sealing the railway's fate.

In June 1958 the railway celebrated its bicentenary with a special passenger train from Moor Road to Broom Pit and back. This event aroused considerable local interest and, in September 1959, the Leeds University Union Railway Society resolved to attempt to acquire the railway as a working museum. This resulted in the creation of the Middleton Railway Preservation Society under the leadership of Dr R.F. Youell.

The Preservation Era

On 18 June 1960 the preservationists re-opened the line by running a diesel-hauled special. There was no intention to operate the railway on a regular basis but two firms, Robinson & Birdsell and Clayton, agreed to patronise the railway and so a daily diesel-hauled service was introduced. The Middleton Railway acquired another first, the first preserved railway to operate a commercial goods service and so became the first standard-gauge railway to be taken over and operated by unpaid volunteers. Initially passenger services only operated for one week, using an ex-Swansea and Mumbles Railway double-deck tram. Regular operation of passenger trains began in 1969 using one of the steam or diesel locomotives. Passengers were carried in open wagons until two PMV 4-wheel vans were converted to coaches reminiscent of those used by collieries. The volunteers continued to operate a freight service until 1983.

The railway is home to a representative selection of locomotives built by the famous Leeds manufacturers of John Fowler, Hudswell Clarke, the Hunslet Engine Co. and Manning Wardle. The railway was closed in 2005, the first time in its history, as the Heritage Lottery Trust granted the Middleton Railway an award of £737,000 to create better visitor and education facilities at their Moor Road–Hunslet site. This was to ensure that more people could see the railway's historic collection of locomotives and learn more about their local heritage and the heritage of the railway.

The railway currently operates passenger services over approximately 1 mile of track from Moor Road, to Park Halt, which is on the outskirts of Middleton Park. The railway hopes to extend the line so that it terminates near the park amenities and discussions are ongoing with Leeds City Council to work towards this aim.

Ex-Bynes Steel Ltd and ex-Swansea & Mumbles Railway 0-6-0ST *Swansea* (Avonside No.1506 of 1906) is pictured on 2 July 1966 in seemingly derelict condition. Although in possession of a number of industrial steam engines the railway used diesels to work its important revenue earning freight services.

In August 1975 we see Bagnall 0-4-0ST *Matthew Murray* of 1943 (ex-Cohens of Stanningley) waiting at Park Gates with a return working to Moor Road. The passenger accommodation is the five-plank open wagon. At this time the railway's passenger service was rather basic.

On 21 July 2002 Hudswell Clarke 0-6-0T Manchester Ship Canal Railway No.67 of 1921 runs into Moor Road station with a train from Park Gates. The passenger accommodation is now two converted 4-wheel PMVs, a considerable improvement on the open wagons of earlier days.

A general view of Moor Road station taken on Sunday 21 July 2002. The workshops are to the left while other rolling stock is stabled in the sidings to the right. MSC 0-6-0T No.67 has run round and waits with the next train to Park Gates. This tank engine was initially preserved on the Keighley & Worth Valley Railway where it starred in BBC TV's 1967 adaptation of *The Railway Children*.

The new Heritage Lottery Fund sponsored new headquarters, and the museum building at Moor Road is seen on a dull Sunday, 21 May 2006. On the right Manning Wardle 0-6-0ST *Matthew Murray* of 1903 is seen raising steam ready to work the day's passenger trains.

A close up of the Middleton Railway's two passenger coaches as seen on 21 July 2002. Each vehicle is fitted with slatted seats reminiscent of the type of coaches used by collieries to transport miners to and from the pit-heads and most appropriate for an ex-colliery line.

As the Middleton Railway's mainline leaves Moor Road it immediately tunnels under the M621 motorway. The site here is surrounded by high security fencing as this part of south Leeds is particularly prone to the attention of thieves and vandals. Some of the railway's goods stock is visible in this view from 21 May 2006.

The inside of the Middleton Railway's new exhibition room shows what a significant facility this is as it is capable of housing up to a dozen locomotives. Nearest the camera is *Mirvale*, a Hudswell Clarke 0-4-0ST built in 1955. *Mirvale* was originally preserved on the North York Moors Railway where, although it was steamed, it proved to be too small and so found a new home at the Middleton Railway.

Manchester Ship Canal No.67 is a large tank engine by Middleton Railway standards and is easily able to cope with the two-coach trains regularly run. However, it is entirely appropriate that it should be preserved here in the Hunslet district of Leeds close to where it was built in 1921.

Journey's end – Manning Wardle 0-6-0ST is seen at Park Gates on a very wet Sunday, 21 May 2006, about to run round its train. This tank engine is the second locomotive to carry the name *Matthew Murray* on the Middleton Railway as it was thought appropriate to keep the name of one of the nineteenth-century pioneers of the use of steam engines on the railway in the public eye.

two

The Keighley
& Worth Valley
Railway

The mill town of Keighley was joined to the expanding rail network on 16 March 1847 with the opening of the Leeds & Bradford Extension Railway. Taken over by the Midland Railway in August 1852 Keighley was regarded as the rail-head for the Worth and Bridgehouse valley mills and their insatiable appetite for raw materials. Wanting to reduce overheads the mill owners were soon involved in drawing up a number of schemes to build a railway between Oxenhope, Haworth and Keighley.

The efforts of 1845 and 1853 came to nothing but in 1861 John McLandsborough's plans were submitted to Parliament and gained the Royal Assent on 30 June 1862. The authorised railway was engineered to leave Keighley station in a south-easterly direction but in order to follow the Worth Valley it immediately climbed at 1 in 58 on a 9-chain curve to head south-west to Ingrow, Damens, Oakworth, Haworth and Oxenhope where it was to terminate near the junction of Weasel Lane and Moor House Lane.

The ceremonial cutting of the first sod took place on 9 February 1864 but owing to difficulties with Ingrow tunnel it was not until the autumn of 1866 that works trains were able to work along the complete 4 miles between Keighley and Oxenhope. The principal civil engineering works were the 120ft bridge over the River Worth at Keighley, Ingrow tunnel and Vale Mill Viaduct, a 30 span wooden trestle viaduct that carried the railway over the River Worth and a mill dam at Oakworth. Before the railway could open, violent storms on 14 November 1866 undermined many of the embankments and cuttings and the resultant remedial work meant that the official opening had to be put back to Saturday 13 April 1867.

All did not go well as the opening train stalled on the 1 in 58 gradient out of Keighley but as was the custom on these occasions congratulatory speeches were followed by a repast of good food. The first day of normal services, Monday 15 April, saw a timetable of six return passenger workings in place with two on Sundays. Within six months the Sunday service had been increased to four return workings. Interestingly the first train of the day started from Oxenhope, necessitating the working of an early morning empty train up the branch.

The important goods traffic was well looked after as the Midland Railway guaranteed that any goods delivered to any of the stations before 10a.m. would be delivered to any address in the West Riding the same day. The railway also brought with it the delivery of much cheaper coal which benefited both domestic and industrial users and also allowed both Haworth and Oakworth to build their own gasworks.

In 1869 a small engine shed was built on the Skipton side of Keighley station to house the branch engine. The line to Oxenhope, however, was not easy to work as it possessed no intermediate passing loops and on 9 September 1875 the 6.15a.m. pick-up goods and empty coaching stock ran away downhill from Oakworth and smashed into a passenger train at Keighley, causing fourteen casualties. A new station was opened at Keighley in July 1878 to accommodate the Great Northern Railway's new Keighley-Queensbury-Bradford and Halifax lines.

By 1875 the branch was worked by Johnson 0-6-0Ts and with the advent of heavier trains the condition of Vale Mill Viaduct was giving rise to concern about its stability as the foundations appeared to be shifting. Plans were drawn up to replace it by a three-arch stone viaduct and 73-yard-long long tunnel and the new deviation was brought into use on Sunday 6 November 1892. The last decade of the nineteenth century brought further improvements with goods loops and signal boxes being provided at Oakworth and Haworth. Extensions to the station buildings at Haworth, Oakworth and Oxenhope were also put in hand. Such was the traffic on offer that by the summer of 1903 no less than sixteen passenger trains were run over the branch every weekday with a six on a Sunday.

The 1923 Grouping saw little change on the branch as Midland 0-6-0Ts and 0-6-0 tender locomotives remained the usual motive power. In 1935 when Keighley shed became a sub-shed to Skipton, push-pull passenger trains were introduced powered by Johnson 1P 0-4-4Ts. Traffic was still buoyant because in 1938 there were seventeen daily departures from Keighley and nineteen from Oxenhope. This did not continue for long, however, as the outbreak of war in September 1939 curtailed many services. The return of peace in 1945 saw services pruned to half the pre-war level and on 21 May 1949 the tiny station at Damens was closed.

With nationalisation new Ivatt 2MT 2-6-2Ts started working the passenger trains and eventually they replaced the Johnson 0-4-4Ts. In 1956 three-coach push-pull trains made up of gangwayed stock were introduced, worked by Ivatt or Riddles 2-6-2Ts. The goods workings, however, still remained the province of the 3F 0-6-0s. The midday non-push-pull trains saw Ivatt 4MT 2-6-0s and Fairburn 2-6-4Ts working up to Oxenhope.

The cold wind of change began to be felt in 1955 when the ex-GNR lines to Queensbury closed. At first this brought an increase in goods working on the Worth Valley but the omnipotent lorry and bus services were eating into the railway's traditional sources of traffic. In July 1959 British Railways announced its intention to close the line despite annual passenger figures of 130,000. Given a reprieve diesel multiple units were introduced and peak time traffic increased but BR was determined to close the line and passenger services were regrettably withdrawn on 31 December 1961. Goods working continued until June 1962 and on 18 June 1962 a last passenger train was worked over the line by 3F No.43856.

The Preservation Era

Local people felt that the railway could be saved and run privately and this led to a public meeting being held in Keighley on 24 January 1962. Such was the support that a further meeting on 1 March resolved to form a preservation society with the aim of re-opening the line from Keighley to Oxenhope, so the Keighley & Worth Valley Preservation Society came into being.

It was hoped to rent the line from BR and raise finance by operating a freight service. Unfortunately BR withdrew the freight services and announced that it wanted an outright sale of the branch. After much negotiating BR finally agreed to the Society buying the line from Bridge 5 to Oxenhope for £34,000, to be paid over a twenty-five-year period. In April 1966 BR allowed the purchase of the Worth Valley side of Keighley station. The contract with BR for the sale was finally signed on 6 April 1967, leaving the only obstacle to re-opening the branch the acquisition of a Light Railway Order. This was acquired by BR on 16 October 1967 and transferred to the Worth Valley Co. on 27 May 1968. After an official inspection of the line and its rolling stock on 8 June the date of the re-opening was set for 29 June 1968.

The first public train run by the KWVRPS departed from Keighley station at 2.35p.m. hauled by Ivatt '2MT' 2-6-2T No.41241, painted in crimson-lake livery and lettered K&WVR, and 'USA' 0-6-0T No.72, painted in golden brown with a silver smokebox. Services were initially confined to weekends with diesel railbuses working the early morning trains and steam trains taking over in the early afternoon. The winter service quickly dwindled to a small locomotive and a single coach. In 1969 the railway's fortunes began to rise as more people became aware of its existence. By 1970, ways were being sought to increase the branch's operating capacity. More coaches and larger locomotives arrived but it was not until a loop was laid at Damens in 1971 that the line's capacity was radically altered.

The decade after re-opening saw the railway gradually find it feet and develop into a major tourist attraction. In 1970, the year when the railway had been used by EMI to film Edith Nesbitt's classic story *The Railway Children*, 71,000 passengers were carried. Such was the interest in the film that in 1971 125,000 passengers were carried. Oakworth station, where much of the film was shot, became the winner of the 'Best preserved Station' award. To cope with this increase in traffic ex-mainline locomotives arrived, often from Barry scrapyard, for restoration. More coaches were acquired from BR.

Gradually Haworth yard and goods shed were converted into a comprehensive workshop and engine shed facility. Oxenhope was likewise developed as the carriage and wagon workshops of the railway and a small museum was also established here. All of the stations received much needed maintenance with the exception of Ingrow. The buildings there were derelict and the decision was taken to replace them with those from the closed station at Foulridge on the disused Skipton to Colne line. Much time and labour was expended on bringing the track into a first class state. At Ingrow the Vintage Carriage Trust established its headquarters and museum and it was here that the Bahamas Locomotive Society developed its own workshops after their base at Dinting was closed.

After a serious decline in passenger numbers the railway has recently seen its fortunes on the rise. The decision to abandon its original house liveries – engines in liveries never carried before and coaches in primrose and blue livery – led to the branch being marketed as an example of a BR branch set in the London Midland Region of the 1950s. Authentic liveries for locomotives, rolling stock and stations have given the railway a distinctive niche in the preserved steam railway market, one that it is making very much its own.

Keighley station on 17 October 1946 finds LNER 'N1' Class 0-6-2T No.9449 having just arrived from Bradford via Queensbury with the 12.10p.m. all stations local in platform 4 while LMS 0-4-4T No.1275 is waiting in platform 3 with the Oxenhope push-pull train The ex-GNR route from Keighley to Bradford and Halifax was closed in 1955 while BR withdrew the Worth Valley passenger trains on New Year's Eve, 31 December 1961. (H.C. Casserley)

The Worth Valley branch shares Keighley station with Network Rail, the old BR. Platforms 1 and 2 serve the Skipton to Shipley mainline while platforms 3 and 4 belong to the Worth Valley. On 1 December 2002 the Worth Valley's Class 108 diesel multiple unit has just arrived from Oxenhope and is occupying platform 4.

When the Bahamas Railway Society relocated from Dinting to Ingrow they brought with them the preserved LNWR Webb 'Coal Tank' No.1054. Here the 1888 built 0-6-2T is seen making a spirited departure from Keighley with a short working to Ingrow on 20 March 1993. Although the Worth Valley is an ex-Midland Railway branch the LNWR tank engine looks at home framed by the Midland water tank.

When the opportunity to acquire the disused turntable from Garsdale on the Settle & Carlisle line arose the KWVR stepped in and brought it to Keighley. Although only capable of turning the railway's smaller locomotives it does enable stock to be turned to even out tyre wear. On 3 May 1998 ex-GWR '5700' 0-6-0PT No.5775 is pictured on the turntable awaiting its next working.

Worth Valley trains face a difficult start out of Keighley with the 1 in 58 gradient starting at the end of the platforms and the line also curving sharply to the right. In the summer of 1951 a Johnson 0-4-4T is pictured propelling the branch line's push-pull set into Keighley. To the left can be seen the turntable pit and both lines have checkrails because of the severity of the curve. (R.S. Carpenter Photos)

Since re-opening in 1968, the Worth Valley has seen a number of Stanier 'Black Five' 4-6-0s at work. Home-based No.45212 has at various times been joined by Nos 45025, 45305 and 45407. Pictured at Keighley on 10 October 2002, masquerading as No.45157 *The Glasgow Highlander*, is Ian Riley's No.45407.

Ingrow is the first station along the branch from Keighley and on 24 April 1954 Ivatt '2MT' 2-6-2T No.41325 is seen propelling the 9.40a.m. from Oxenhope toward Keighley. Today Ingrow is the base for both the Vintage Carriage Trust and the Bahamas Railway Society. When the Worth Valley re-opened in 1968 Ingrow station was in a derelict state and has now been replaced by the ex-Midland building from Foulridge on the Skipton to Colne line. (H.C. Casserley)

Thanks to the efforts of the Vintage Carriage Trust the KWVR's ex-Metropolitan Railway coaches have gradually been restored as near as is possible to their original state. Looking absolutely magnificent in varnished teak livery at Keighley station on 19 September 1998 are three of these historic coaches waiting to form a vintage train working up the valley.

Contrasts in motive power at Keighley 1 – here we see two BR classes in action on 3 May 1998 during the railway's 'BR Standard Gala'. Class '2MT' 2-6-0 No.78022 is piloting visiting Class '4MT' 4-6-0 No.75019 (the real No.75014) while on the turntable road is LNWR 'Coal Tank' No.1054.

Contrasts in motive power at Keighley 2 – *Bellerophon*, the KWVR's Haydock Foundry 0-6-0WT of 1874, is pictured leaving Keighley with a vintage shuttle for Ingrow on 19 September 1998. *Bellerophon* was one of the many industrial locomotives that arrived at Haworth in the early days of the preserved railway. At the time of writing it is on the Foxfield Railway where it is being overhauled.

Running in its *Railway Children* livery '5700' 0-6-0PT No.5775 is seen running into Ingrow station on 24 September 1972 with a train for Oxenhope. In its early years the railway coach behind the pannier tank is one such example having been given an attractive primrose and blue paint scheme.

The station at Damens, deep in the valley of the River Worth and the smallest in England, is seen here in 1974 as the KWVR's '5700' 0-6-0PT, now running as London Transport No.L89, drifts into the station. The London Transport livery illustrated here is an authentic one for this engine as it was bought from London Transport in working order.

The loop at Damens was laid in 1971 and immediately increased the number of trains that could be timetabled. The rural aspect of this part of the Worth Valley is illustrated by this view of 0-6-0ST No.62 as it powers through the loop heading for Oakworth while 'Black Five' No.5025 waits to continue its tender first journey downhill to Ingrow and Keighley.

The unrelenting gradient from Keighley to Oxenhope means that the Worth Valley's engines have to be worked hard. On 27 July 2002 Taff Vale Railway 0-6-2T No.85 has steam to spare as it climbs away from Damens Loop towards Oakworth station. Once above Damens the industrial environs of Keighley are left behind and the railway runs through some spectacular Pennine scenery.

The station yard at Oakworth has been developed as the railway's permanent way depot. On 27 July 2002 Hudswell Clarke 0-6-0DM No.D2511 is busy shunting the yard. Oakworth yard and station were featured extensively in the EMI film *The Railway Children* and the restored Midland station has won a number of prestigious awards.

On 15 July 1972 'Black Five' 4-6-0 No.5025 is pictured on the approach to Oakworth station with an Oxenhope train. The point in the foreground provides access to the goods yard. No.5025 arrived on the railway as No.45025 and was restored to LMS livery, remaining on the KWVR until the Strathspey Railway was open and able to provide covered accommodation.

The picturesque setting of Oakworth station is seen on 27 July 2002. The stone buildings blend into the background and it is almost possible to hear the rails groaning as they expand under the unrelenting sun and smell the creosote of the sleepers. The building to the right is the goods shed.

Mytholmes tunnel is the setting as Standard '4MT' Class 2-6-4T No.80002 heads from Oakworth towards Haworth on 24 September 1972. No.80002, after being returned to steam, spent almost two decades out of traffic with firebox problems. Eventually a new steel firebox was fitted and since then the big 2-6-4T has proved to be the ideal motive power for the branch, being both powerful and economical.

On 24 April 1954 Ivatt '2MT' 2-6-2T No.41325 is seen propelling the branch push-pull set out of Haworth station towards Keighley. Haworth became the headquarters of the KVWR and has been restored to a high standard. The railway's main shop is here and the profits from the sales of books, DVDs, postcards and models are all ploughed back into the railway. (H.C. Casserley)

Left: Worth Valley super power. On 30 March 1974 the NRM's Standard Class '9F' 2-10-0 No.92220 *Evening Star*, the last steam locomotive to be built by BR, has just arrived at Haworth with a BBC Radio Blackburn 'Steam Up Special'. While No.92220 was on loan to the railway it showed complete mastery of all the trains it worked and made some of the fastest and most surefooted departures from Keighley.

Opposite below: The goods shed in Haworth yard became the locomotive workshops for the KWVR. In this mid-1970 view some idea of the basic facilities can be gained. 'WD' 2-8-0 No.1931 is heading for Oxenhope while ex-Midland Railway '4F' 0-6-0 No.43924 is stabled in the yard. Inside the shed can be seen English Electric shunter No.D0226. No.1931 is at the time of writing nearing the end of a rebuild which will see it assume a BR-style identity as No.90733.

Above: Ivatt Class '2MT' 2-6-2T No.41241 is seen leaving Haworth with a train for Oxenhope on 20 October 1968. The engine is painted in Midland Railway crimson and carries the legend K&WVR on its side tanks. Another class of engine that was to prove ideal for the operating needs of the newly preserved railway, No.41241, was bought out of traffic from BR when it was allocated to nearby Skipton shed.

One of the first engines to arrive at Haworth before the railway was re-opened was Gresley 'N2' Class 0-6-2T No.69523 which was initially restored as LNER No.4744. Owned by the Gresley Society the 'N2' moved to the Great Central Railway at Loughborough. On 18 September 1998 we see the resplendent No.69523 in Haworth yard having returned to the railway for an autumn gala event.

In the quest to provide the KWVR with engines capable of working five and six coach trains an ex-USA Transportation Corps 2-8-0 was acquired from Poland. Restored to working order No.5820 is seen in Haworth yard in May 1980 being prepared for its next duty in the company of 'West Country' Pacific No.34092 *City of Wells*. No.5820 was the American equivalent of the British 'WD' 2-8-0s seen previously.

The Worth Valley has gained an enviable reputation for its gala events when visiting locomotives provide the magnet that can draw in huge crowds. On 15 April 1994 we see visiting 'Manor' Class 4-6-0 No.7828 *Odney Manor* shunting the Worth Valley's resident Stanier '8F' 2-8-0 No.48431 and another visitor, 'S15' Class 4-6-0 No.E828, just outside of Haworth yard. The railway at this point crosses Bridgehouse Beck which has been known to flood the railway. The line to the right is the 'mainline' to Oxenhope.

The 1.15p.m. from Keighley has just arrived at the southern terminus of Oxenhope on 17 October 1946 behind Johnson '1P' 0-4-4T No.1275. This locomotive, a Worth Valley regular, was one of sixty-two members of this class that were taken into BR stock on 1 January 1948 and allocated the numbers 58030–58091. (H.C. Casserley)

A deserted Oxenhope station provides the setting for this picture of Ivatt '2MT' 2-6-2T No.41325 with push-pull set M19382 and M24325 which has just arrived with the 9.15a.m. from Keighley on 24 April 1954. Such has been the development here that the fields in the background are now covered with residential housing and the station itself has also been extensively altered. (R.M. Casserley)

Twenty-four years separate this photograph from the one above. On Sunday, 2 February 1970 'USA' Class 0-6-0T No.72 arrives at Oxenhope with a short working from Haworth comprising a Bulleid compartment coach and an ex-NER bogie saloon. No.72 is in light brown livery with WORTH VALLEY on its side tanks and has a silver painted smokebox in American fashion. The white shed visible to the right and the water tank at the end of the platform were both erected by KWVR volunteers.

We move on to Saturday 27 May 1973 as '5700' 0-6-0PT No.5775 leaves Oxenhope with a train for Keighley. The engine is in *Railway Children* livery and carries WORTH VALLEY on its pannier tanks. The yard, which here is occupied by a caravan and Roberts Sheffield tramcar, is now the site of the KWVR's carriage depot and museum.

The largest tank engines used by BR on the branch were the Fairburn '4MT' 2-6-4Ts and here we see No.42138 having arrived from Keighley on a sunny 10 October 1956. When engines of this class were used, as they were not push-pull fitted, they had to run round their coaches and would haul the train bunker-first down into Keighley. Although the KWVR does not own a Fairburn tank engine it does possess BR Standard No.80002 which is the Riddles development of the Fairburn design. (R.S. Carpenter Photos)

For many years the Worth Valley relied heavily upon a number of 0-6-0STs to maintain its services. Here entering Oxenhope on 31 March 1973 is *Fred*, a Robert Stephenson & Hawthorn 0-6-0ST built in 1950. The engine carries a very attractive blue livery with WORTH VALLEY on the saddle tank sides. As trains grew heavier the 0-6-0STs struggled to keep time and were eventually replaced by larger locomotives. *Fred* has now left the railway.

Newly restored, and yet to be fitted with its nameplates, 'West Country' Pacific No.34092 *City of Wells* is being run-in as the pilot engine to 'USA' Class 0-6-0T No.72 and is seen having just arrived at Oxenhope in October 1979. No.34092 arrived at Ingrow from Barry scrapyard in November 1971 and has been used on the mainline where it proved itself to be a powerful and reliable machine.

On 8 August 2002 ex-LMS '3F' 0-6-0T No.47279 arrives at Oxenhope with a midweek service train. The KWVR now markets the railway as a 1950s branch line on the LMR and this picture shows just how effective this has been. No.47279 is in immaculate condition at the head of a rake of maroon-painted BR Mark I stock. The railway has come a long way from when engines and rolling stock were painted in 'house' liveries.

End of the line as '3F' 0-6-0T No.47279 runs round its train at Oxenhope on 8 August 2002. The parachute water tank has replaced the first water tank built at the opposite end of Oxenhope station back in the 1960s. Since the early days the headshunt here has been extended and a picnic site has been developed to the left of the Midland Railway-style fencing.

A last look at one of the railway's smallest engines at work in April 1979. Ex-Manchester Ship Canal Railway Hudswell Clarke 0-6-0T No.31 *Hamburg* makes a spirited departure from Keighley during an Enthusiasts Weekend. Waiting in the loop for its next train is 'USA' Class 0-6-0T No.72. Neither engine seen here is in traffic at the time of writing as both require major overhauls.

One of the locomotives that made the KWVR famous – ex-GWR '5700' Class 0-6-0T seen in Haworth yard on 15 June 1970 in its fictitious *Railway Children* livery as a GNSR engine. When freshly applied the tan-coloured paint looked smart and the publicity generated by the film was a welcome boost to the railway.

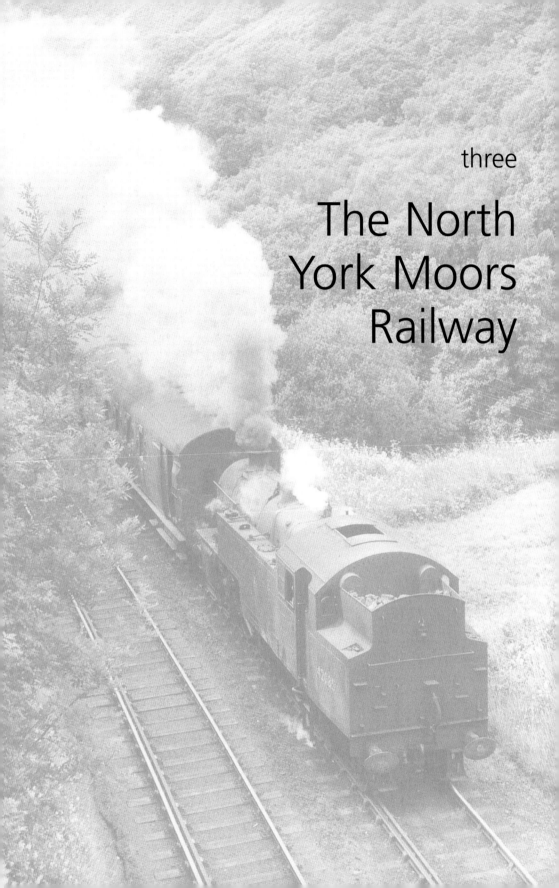

three

The North York Moors Railway

The North York Moors Railway is one of the most successful preserved railways in the country, regularly carrying in excess of 300,000 passengers a year. It also passes through some of the most starkly beautiful countryside – the 1000ft-high sandstone and limestone plateau of the North York Moors – that was sculptured by the glaciers of the last Ice Age.

The railway's origins date from 1832 when George Stephenson reported on the feasibility of a line from Whitby to Pickering. Parliamentary consent was gained on 16 May 1833 and work commenced in October. The first section of line opened between Whitby and Whinstone Dyke, south of Grosmont tunnel, on Friday 15 May 1835 and was worked by horses. A year later on 26 May 1836 the railway opened to Pickering, again using horses. The principal feature of the line was the 1,500-yard inclined plane between Beck Hole and Goathland. The initial service comprised two return passenger trains a day, Sundays excepted.

When the 5-mile branch from Malton to Pickering was opened on 7 July 1845, steam engines were used making the Whitby to Pickering's use of horses appear archaic. Before the horses could be replaced by steam power the line had to be significantly upgraded. The work involved laying double track capable of carrying the increased weight of the iron horses. The wooden viaducts over the River Esk were replaced by iron structures and a new Grosmont tunnel was constructed. The inclined plane was updated by installing a stationary steam engine.

In 1854 the Whitby & Pickering Railway became part of the newly created North Eastern Railway. The inclined plane was viewed with distaste and steps were taken to replace it with a 4-mile deviation. Engineered with a ruling gradient of 1 in 49, the new line began just north of Grosmont tunnel and rejoined the original line at Moorgates, some 1 mile south of Goathland and the line's summit. A new station was also provided at Goathland.

To work passenger trains over the line the NER built a number of small-wheeled 4-4-0s to the design of Edward Fletcher which quickly acquired the sobriquet 'Whitby Bogies'. Goods traffic was handled by various examples of 0-6-0s. At the beginning of the twentieth century there were six passenger trains running each way between Whitby, Pickering and Malton with one Sunday working. Goods services comprised two daily workings which started at opposite ends of the line.

The outbreak of war in August 1914 brought the end of the summer only Whitby to Beck Hole workings. The line was also singled between New Bridge and Levisham to release track materials for the army in France. When the NER became part of the LNER group in 1923 there were only five passenger trains in each direction. These trains were by now worked by a number of different types, 'F8' 2-4-2Ts, 'G5' 0-4-4Ts and 'A6' 4-6-2Ts with 'J23' and 'J24' 0-6-0s handling the goods traffic. Although the basic pattern of passenger and goods workings remained the same additional trains were added to the summer timetables.

From 1932, in an attempt to introduce more economical workings, the LNER used some of its Sentinel steam railcars on the Whitby to Goathland and Malton to Whitby local passenger workings. The 1930s also saw the LNER introduce camping coaches at Goathland and Levisham as well as running 'Scenic Excursions' over the line in summer. However, all these initiatives came to nothing in September 1939 when war was declared against Germany and the services were severely rationalised.

After the war camping coaches, the scenic excursion and through coaches from London reappeared. 'A8' 4-6-2Ts and 'G5' 0-4-4Ts were still in charge of the passenger traffic while 'J24', 'J27' and 'J39' 0-6-0s handled the goods workings. With nationalisation further classes appeared, most notably the 'L1' 2-6-4Ts, Ivatt 2-6-0s and 2-6-2Ts, Fairburn 2-6-4Ts and Riddles Standard '3MT' 2-6-2Ts and 2-6-0s while 'B1' 4-6-0s were used on through trains. Although Metro-Cammell diesel multiple units were introduced on some of the passenger workings in 1958 most of the trains remained steam powered.

Despite its value during the summer months the Beeching Report recommended that the line should be closed. It was claimed that the line was losing £50,000 a year, a sum not accepted locally. The last official BR workings occurred on 6 March 1965. However, in November the line briefly re-opened between Whitby and Goathland when all the local roads were blocked by snow. By September 1967, when it looked as if track-lifting would soon begin, the embryonic North York Moors Railway stepped in and set in motion what was to become one of the most successful preservation schemes in the country.

The Preservation Era

A preliminary appraisal of what was required to save the Grosmont to Pickering line suggested that an asking price of £100,000 would be placed on the 18-mile line. In discussion with British Railways the newly formed North Yorkshire Moors Railway Co. agreed a purchase price of £35,000 for the 6-mile section from Grosmont to Ellerbeck and a further £7,500 for the railway property between Grosmont and High Mill near Pickering. The original intention had been to create a terminus at Ellerbeck close to the Pickering to Whitby road with the long-term goal of re-opening through to Pickering.

In 1968 BR accepted that the NYMR was serious in its intentions to re-open the line and agreed in principle to the sale of the line and structures. This allowed the first train to run under the auspices of the NYMR on 2 February 1969 when 0-4-0ST *Mirvale* steamed from Pickering to Grosmont where it was stabled inside Grosmont tunnel alongside the four-wheel diesel railbus No.79978. However, it was to be April 1973 before public services commenced. In the interim period both the North Riding County Council and the North Yorkshire Moors National Park Committee made it known that they were not keen on attracting large numbers of cars to Ellerbeck. Instead they agreed to buy the 12 miles of track from Ellerbeck to Pickering providing that the NYMR was prepared to operate between Pickering and Grosmont from the outset. Faced with tackling a project larger than anticipated the railway nevertheless decided to fall in with the wishes of the two authorities.

The railway was then faced with the problem of how to run an 18-mile line. The solution was determined by their then meagre resources. There just were not sufficient locomotive and carriages to run a full-scale steam railway to and from Pickering. Additionally there was no passing loop at Levisham and there was not a proper station at Pickering. Consequently when the railway was opened to the public on 22 April 1973 steam trains ran daily between Grosmont and Goathland with a diesel multiple unit working between Goathland and Pickering at weekends. These trains did not actually run into Pickering station because of a dispute between the local council and railway over the station site. The council wanted to redevelop the site but with the backing of the County Council the station was saved.

During the 1974 season the diesel unit operated to and from Pickering on every running day. The use of the dmu was marketed in a positive vein as a 'National Park Scenic Cruise'. The long hot summer of 1976 was to have seen two Sunday steam trips over the whole line but the risk of fire in Newtondale meant the railway had to search for an alternative form of motive power. This appeared in the shape of a Class 24 diesel No D5032. For the first time the NYMR had an effective locomotive to work to and from Pickering. Unfortunately the general public preferred to be pulled by a steam locomotive. Steam is more expensive to operate and maintain than diesel but steam attracts more passengers. To run more steam trains better facilities were required along with more steam locomotives.

In 1980 some 43 per cent of passenger trains were steam-hauled. Most of the service was kept going by the Class 24 diesel, the National Railway Museum's Class 31 No.D5500, whose three-year loan was about to expire, and the dmu. The following year the season opened with the railway having only two serviceable steam locomotives. Fortunately matters improved as an influx of privately owned mainline steam and diesel locomotives arrived on the railway. By 1986 timetabled diesel operation had been reduced to the first train of the day out of Pickering, and within three years even this had disappeared.

To service and overhaul its fleet of locomotives a fully equipped workshop and engine shed has been built at Grosmont. Facilities have also been provided to store undercover engines awaiting their turn to be overhauled. At the same time Pickering goods yard has been developed as a carriage workshop. At Grosmont camping coaches have been re-introduced and much of the stock stored over the years has been moved elsewhere. Great steps have been made to maintain and improve the track and signalling. There have, of course, been set-backs – flooding at Pickering and land slips on the moors – but it is safe to say that the NYMR has not been in such a good state for many decades. Passenger figures of 300,000 or more a year make it the envy of many other preserved railways. Its gala events such as the annual '1940s Weekend' have won plaudits from across the country. Not content to sit on its laurels, the railway is actively pursuing its goal to run steam trains back into the historic holiday resort of Whitby.

Goathland in June 1934 finds Stirling ex-Hull & Barnsley Railway Class 'J23' 0-6-0 No.2453 at the head of a freight train at Goathland. The 'J23s' were all scrapped between 1925 and 1938. Although much has changed, this scene is still recognisable today. (R.S. Carpenter Photos)

An engineer's train is pictured near Levisham station *c.*1934 in charge of an ex-Hull & Barnsley Railway Class 'J23' 0-6-0. This view was taken facing Levisham and again the location has not changed significantly in the intervening years. (R.S. Carpenter Photos)

On 31 March 1953 ex-LNER Class 'J25' 0-6-0 No.65656 is seen at Pickering on a pick-up goods working alongside the ex-NER engine shed. In the background is Pickering station. The 'J25s' were a Worsdell design built for the NER between 1898 and 1902 and although the first of the class was withdrawn in 1933 the last went to the scrap merchants as late as 1962. (J.W. Armstrong/Kidderminster Railway Museum)

The 4p.m. Malton to Whitby Town, which also conveyed carriages from the 11.28a.m. ex–King's Cross, is seen arriving at Goathland station on Friday 25 July 1958 behind ex-LNER Class 'A8' 4-6-2T No.69886. These big tank engines saw a lot of use over what is now the NYMR and unfortunately all of the 'A8s' were withdrawn before the preservation movement got under way. (Michael Mensing)

On 1 August 1958 we see two three-car sets of Metro Cammell diesel multiple units emerging from Grosmont tunnel while working the 1.20p.m. Goathland to Whitby service. Although the brand new units brought higher passenger figures these were insufficient to prevent the Beeching cuts badly affecting the railway network in this part of Yorkshire. (Michael Mensing)

In August 1958 we see Fairburn '4MT' Class 2-6-4T No.42084 departing from Grosmont with a train bound for Malton via Pickering. The fireman has built up his fire ready for the 1 in 49 climb to Goathland. From this angle the railway here has changed little in the intervening fifty years. (Michael Mensing)

The NYMR has run steam trains back to Whitby Town and has recreated this scene at Ruswarp using the railway's own BR Standard Class '4MT' 2-6-4T No.80135. In 1957 we see classmate No.80118 running into Ruswarp station on the line between Grosmont and Whitby. (Michael Mensing)

Above: Whitby Town station on Saturday, 2 August 1958 finds ex–LNER 'A8' Class 4-6-2T No.69864 shunting two vans into the centre road. It is not possible to recreate this view today as the station has been radically rationalised, but at least trains still serve this historic holiday resort. (Michael Mensing)

Left: For many years the NYMR relied on relatively small tank engines to maintain the steam service on the railway. One of the engines that was used and has now moved on is Ivatt 'J52' 0-6-0ST No.1247 (ex-BR No.68846) seen here at Goathland. The engine is carrying fully lined out GNR green and at the time of writing is on display at Locomotion – The NRM at Shildon.

The need to provide a covered workshop was an urgent necessity and so a two-road shed was built at Grosmont. Seen outside are Ivatt 'J52' No.1247, ex-Lambton Colliery Kitson 0-6-2T No.29 (Works No.4263 of 1904), ex-NER Raven 'T2' Class 0-8-0 No.2238 (BR Class 'Q6' No.63395) and BR Standard Class '4MT' 2-6-4T No.80135.

In the early days of the NYMR railway revival the Goathland to Pickering section was worked by this AC Cars Ltd four-wheel diesel railbus No.79978, which is seen at Pickering station. Painted in an attractive light green and cream livery the railbus could only carry forty-six passengers and was found to be woefully inadequate at peak periods and was eventually replaced by a conventional diesel multiple unit.

The railway possesses two ex-Lambton Colliery 0-6-2Ts and pictured passing the engine shed and works at Grosmont in May 1980 is Robert Stephenson No.5 (Works No.3377 of 1909). In the yard are Ivatt 'J52' No.1247 and four-wheel railbus No.79978. Before reaching Goathland No.5 is faced with the severe 1 in 49 climb which starts here. The first coach is a BR Mark I high capacity suburban compartment vehicle.

Approaching Pickering station on 12 May 2002 is 'Black Five' Class 4-6-0 No.44767 *George Stephenson*. Owned by Ian Storey this locomotive is unique in that it is fitted with outside Stephenson's valve gear. The Stanier 'Black Fives' are in many ways the ideal locomotive for the current size of trains operated by the NYMR. To the left is the carriage department's headquarters.

Leaving Goathland with a train for Pickering on 30 August 1994 is USATC Class S160 2-8-0 No.2253. Goathland is where ITV's popular *Heartbeat* programme is filmed which often features the railway and consequently brings large numbers of visitors to the small moorland village, many of whom travel on the NYMR.

The railway is fortunate in being able to operate the largest of mainline locomotives. Seen at Grosmont on 6 October 2001 are two ex-ECML 4-6-2s; on the left is 'A4' Class No.60007 *Sir Nigel Gresley* waiting to leave with a train to Pickering and on the right is 'A2' No.60532 *Blue Peter* which has just arrived from Pickering.

The wide-open spaces of the North York Moors provide travellers with unrivalled views whatever the season. Here we see ex-Western Region 'Warship' Class B-B diesel-hydraulic No.821 *Greyhound* between Goathland and Levisham. In very dry summers the NYMR uses diesel locomotives to reduce the risk of setting fire to the tinder dry moorland.

An engine that has been used a great deal on the mainline as well as the NYMR is the NELPG's Peppercorn Class 'K1' 2-6-0 No.62005 seen here between Goathland and Levisham. This powerful mogul is ideally suited to the rigours of working between Grosmont and Pickering as well as, when required, on the Fort William to Mallaig 'Jacobite' trains.

The NYMR's first mainline diesel, Class 24 No.D5032 *Helen Turner*, climbs away from Goathland with a six-coach train bound for Pickering. Bought direct from a scrap merchant the Class 24 has proved to be a valuable asset to the railway. Capable of working both passenger and works trains it is also the ideal stand-by engine.

For a while in the early 1980s the railway had to rely on *Antwerp*, a Hunslet 0-6-0ST (Works No.3180 of 1944), to work its steam services. The 0-6-0ST is pictured in the sylvan setting of the countryside near Goathland as it works a heavy passenger train. The problem with using locomotives such as *Antwerp* is that they have to be worked very hard to keep time and consequently are likely to cause lineside fires.

Above: Another of the NYMR's stalwarts is Stanier 'Black Five' 4-6-0 No.45428 *Eric Tracey* seen here powering away from Goathland with a passenger train for Pickering. At the time of writing No.45428 is in the throws of a heavy overhaul, which includes a complete re-building of the boiler. The railway's steam locomotives are worked hard and consequently have to be maintained in first class condition.

Above: Diesel super-power – 'Deltic' Class Co-Co No.55009 *Alycidon* and 'Warship' No.821 *Greyhound* – stabled at Grosmont. Although neither of these fine locomotives is still on the railway they are a reminder of the variety of motive power that has been used on the railway since its re-opening in 1973.

Right: A long way from its one-time home at 88E Abercynon we find ex-GWR '5600' Class 0-6-2T No.6619 stored in the 'Deviation Shed' at Grosmont awaiting its turn for overhaul on 30 August 1994. This powerful 0-6-2T has proved to be an ideal locomotive for the NYMR and at the time of writing has just returned to steam with a modified Kylchap exhaust system.

Opposite below: Standard Class '4MT' 2-6-4T No.80135 stands over the inspection pit in the workshop at Grosmont in May 1980. In front of the big tank engine can be seen the tender of Southern Railway Class 'S15' 4-6-0 No.841. Although the works are out of bounds for visitors there is a viewing balcony where they can see what work is in progress on the locomotives.

Above: Re-built Bulleid 'West Country' Class Pacific No.34027 *Taw Valley* is pictured passing the sheds at Grosmont with a Pickering bound train on 30 August 1996. The structure to the right is a mechanical coal plant which has eased the coaling of the NYMR's steam locomotives. The privately owned No.34027 is now based on the Severn Valley Railway.

Left: The unmistakable outline of Gresley 'A4' Pacific No.60007 *Sir Nigel Gresley* is pictured at Pickering station. No.60007 is the holder of the post-war speed record for steam locomotives of 112mph and carries plaques on its boiler cladding recording this feat. The world speed record for steam locomotives is held by another 'A4', No.4468 *Mallard*, which touched 126mph in July 1938.

Gala events on the NYMR are invariably busy and on 12 May 2002 ex-GWR '42XX' Class 2-8-0T No.4277 waits for the level crossing gates and signals at Grosmont to clear before setting off with a train for Pickering. Grosmont tunnel can be seen in the distance. Although designed for hauling coal trains in South Wales the big 2-8-0T is quite capable of handling the heaviest trains on the NYMR.

During gala events the NYMR's smaller engines are often used together and here seen entering Pickering station on 12 May 2002 with a working from Grosmont are 0-6-2T No.29 and NELPG owned 'J27' 0-6-0 No.65984. Both these locomotives have been hired by other preserved railways including the Embsay & Bolton Abbey Steam Railway.

To end this look at the NYMR we see two contrasting scenes. Here Stanier 'Black Five' No.5428 is outside the workshop at Grosmont in May 1980. Pictured in LMS livery No.5428 is waiting to be taken into the works for overhaul, after which it was out-shopped in BR livery as No.45428.

Perhaps the most unlikely type of locomotive to work the steeply graded NYMR is a 4-4-0. But Maunsell 'Schools' Class 4-4-0 No.30926 *Repton* has proved to be a most capable and reliable engine. Seen in immaculate condition at Pickering on 12 May 2002 the three-cylinder 4-4-0 seems set to depart for Malton, but unfortunately the line from Pickering has been lifted and so it will run round its train and depart tender first for Goathland and Grosmont.

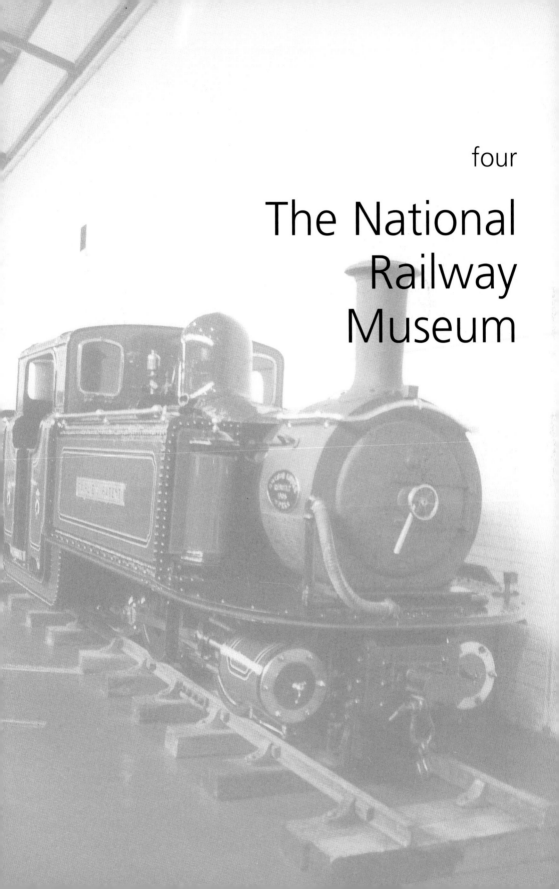

four

The National
Railway
Museum

Opened in 1975 as the successor to the Clapham Transport Museum, the National Railway Museum in York is the world's largest railway museum. Occupying the site of York engine shed (50A), the museum has an unrivalled collection of locomotives, carriages, wagons, artefacts and documents. Special steam events are regularly held and in summer a steam engine is usually to be found giving brake van rides in the yards. A number of the NRM's collection of steam and diesel locomotives are restored to running condition or on loan to preserved railways around the country.

The museum offers visitors three extensive exhibition halls. The Great Hall: the old engine shed, concentrates on the development of railway technology – locomotives, signalling, the Channel tunnel and the Japanese 'Bullet Train'. The museum's workshops form an annexe to the Great Hall. On the opposite side of Leeman Road is the Station Hall which explores the concept of travel by train. Several passenger and freight trains are displayed showing the great diversity of railways from Royal Trains to the humble pick-up goods. The museum's Interactive Learning Centre provides visitors with 'hands-on' experience of the many facets of railway operation.

In the thirty-plus years that the museum has been open it has welcomed in excess of 20 million visitors and in 2001 it was awarded the prestigious 'European Museum of the Year' accolade. In 2004 it also saved the iconic Gresley 'A3' Class Pacific No.4472 *Flying Scotsman* for the nation. Its exhibits range from the world's fastest steam locomotive 'A4' Pacific No.4468 *Mallard* to the diminutive LB&SCR 'Terrier' *Boxhill*, from the prototype *Deltic* diesel electric Co-Co to the Class '02' 0-4-0DH No.D2860 as well as rolling stock from the early nineteenth century through to a Birmingham Airport Maglev passenger car from 1975.

York MPD on 4 April 1967 with Peppercorn 'K1' Class 2-6-0 No.62046 on the left and Thompson 'B1' Class 4-6-0 No.61337 stabled to the right with a Drewry 0-6-0DM shunter. This part of the engine shed was to form the Main Hall of the National Railway Museum. Due to problems with the concrete decaying a new roof had to be built by the museum authorities.

On 4 October 1975 Wainwright SE&CR Class 'D' 4-4-0 No.737 (BR No.31737) was on display in the Main Hall. A careful comparison of the construction of the roof in this photograph and the previous one confirms that this building is indeed the old roundhouse shed of York engine shed.

The prototype English Electric *Deltic* is seen displayed on the main turntable in the Great Hall on 25 October 1993. Originally preserved in the Science Museum in London, *Deltic* was moved to York when the South Kensington museum was re-ordered. At present this locomotive is on display at Barrow Hill near Chesterfield.

Great Western Railway 'Star' Class 4-6-0 No.4003 *Lode Star* looks every inch the thoroughbred that G.J. Churchward intended it to be. The four-cylinder 'Stars' were one of the most significant designs to come out of Swindon Works and influenced the majority of four-cylinder designs that followed during the twentieth century.

The museum also lends some of its exhibits to other museums and centres for special celebratory events. For the 150th anniversary of the opening of the Liverpool and Manchester Railway in 1980, Southern Railway 'Schools' Class 4-4-0 No.925 *Cheltenham* was returned to steam to take part in the grand cavalcade of locomotives at Rainhill. Here No.925 is seen at Bold Colliery where the cavalcade began.

The NRM is very much a 'living' museum and whenever possible has at least one engine in steam to give rides to the visitors who flock to York. Here we see two replica locomotives, *Rocket* in the foreground and the broad gauge 4-2-2 *Iron Duke*, running on the exhibition lines outside the annexe buildings.

One of the NRM's ex-LNER locomotives is 'V2' Class 2-6-2 No.60800 *Green Arrow* pictured here running into Hellifield station after working an excursion south from Carlisle over the S&C. Originally restored as LNER No.4771, at the time of writing *Green Arrow* has just been returned to this condition after running as BR No.60800 for a number of years.

Two of the most recent NRM-owned locomotives to return to steam are seen here at Keighley station on the Keighley & Worth Valley Railway on 14 October 2005 – GWR 'City' Class 4-4-0 No.3440 *City of Truro* and ex-LNWR 'Super D' Class 0-8-0 No.49395. *City of Truro* is reputed to have been the first steam locomotive to run at more than 100mph.

Another Southern Railway locomotive restored to steam was 'King Arthur' Class 4-6-0 No.777 *Sir Lamiel*. Here we see *Sir Lamiel* at Skipton station waiting to take over a 'Cumbrian Mountain Express' working over the Settle & Carlisle Railway on a snowy 2 February 1991. As BR No.30777 this locomotive has just returned to steam on the Great Central Railway.

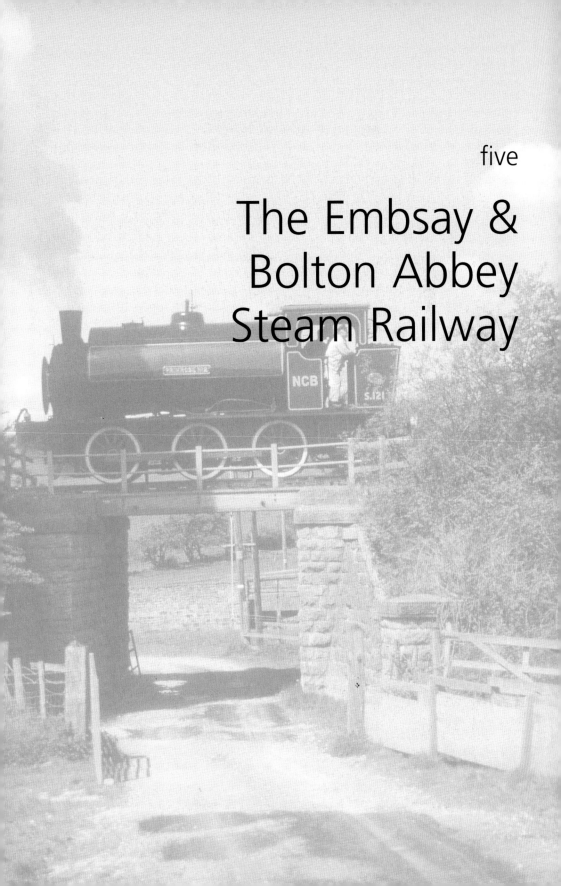

five

The Embsay &
Bolton Abbey
Steam Railway

It was on 1 August 1865 that the Midland Railway and the North Eastern Railway opened their joint line to Ilkley but the line through Embsay to Skipton had to wait until 1 October 1888 to be completed. From Skipton the double-track line turned south, climbing at 1 in 85 before curving over the main Skipton to Carlisle railway, the Keighley Road and the Leeds & Liverpool Canal. Turning to the north-east and still climbing it entered the 219-yard Haw Bank tunnel where the gradient eased to 1 in 90. At Embsay Junction the line to Grassington branched away north-westwards leaving the mainline to turn east towards Embsay.

The station at Embsay was provided with both up and down goods yards and a wooden goods shed. The stone station building was on the up line and a wooden shelter was erected on the down platform. The stationmaster's house was placed at the end of the station drive. A private siding served the Haw Bank Quarry and this was to provide a significant volume of mineral traffic. A standard Midland signal box was built to control the yards and mainlines. Under the stationmaster there was a signalman and three porters who were responsible for local deliveries.

Still heading east the summit of the line was reached at Holywell Bridge, some 4 miles from Skipton, whereupon it descended at 1 in 100 toward Bolton Abbey station. Despite its name this station was a good half hour's walk from the priory it purported to serve. Built on land belonging to the Duke of Devonshire the only railway buildings allowed were the wooden station and houses for the stationmaster and porter. As at Embsay, up and down yards were laid out to serve the nearby Hambleton Quarry. On the up side a siding was provided for the sole use of the Duke of Devonshire.

Leaving Bolton Abbey on a falling gradient and following the valley of the River Wharfe a short climb at 1 in 120 preceded the south-east 1 in 110 descent to Addingham. From Addingham an undulating switchback brought the railway into Ilkley where a girder bridge carried the line over Brook Street into Ilkley station. Beyond Ilkley there were stations at Ben Rhydding and Burley-in-Wharfedale. At the latter a junction took trains to Bradford and Leeds or towards Harrogate and Leeds.

Most of the Midland Railway's passenger trains were handled by Johnson 0-4-4Ts and 2-4-0s while Kirtley and Johnson 0-6-0s dealt with the goods workings. Until August 1914 the NER operated through passenger trains to Bolton Abbey. During the First World War the line between Embsay and Addingham was singled, with the track being requisitioned for use in France. The line remained single until 1921.

The service provided in 1922 comprised five trains each from Leeds and Bradford to Bolton Abbey of which four carried on to Embsay and Skipton. In the up direction there were eight trains from Skipton plus another two from Bolton Abbey, with four going to Leeds and the others to Bradford. The 1923 Grouping saw little change in the working of the railway until the 1930s when competition from motor-buses brought about a reduction in the length of trains and the onset of a slow decline in services. The line did, however, see more than its fair share of Royal Trains as the Duke of Devonshire's grouse moors brought both King George V and King George VI to the estate.

In July 1934 the LMS introduced a camping coach at Bolton Abbey station and camping coaches remained a feature here until 1965 when the station closed. The outbreak of war in September 1939 saw passenger services reduced to just four each way through Embsay. Between 1940 and 1941 Bolton Abbey station yard was taken over by the army as an ammunition dump. The war also saw LNER coke trains from Teeside to Barrow and Workington routed over the line from 20 October 1941. Meanwhile the local pick-up freights and stone trains from the quarries were providing worthwhile volumes of traffic.

In 1946 the LMS and LNER introduced a summer Saturday holiday train between Saltburn and Blackpool. As with the coke trains LNER locomotives came off at Skipton where they were replaced by LMS motive power. In 1948 the coke trains were withdrawn but in their place came ICI ammonia tank workings between Heysham and Haverton Hill. In 1953 these were complemented by oil trains running over the line from Teeside.

The line through Ilkley and Embsay provided an important diversionary route when the Aire Valley line was closed. Consequently there were times when the 'Thames Clyde Express' and the 'Waverley' passed through Embsay behind 'Royal Scot' Class 4-6-0s, 'Britannias' and Gresley 'A3' Pacifics. Unfortunately when Dr Beeching was looking to reduce BR's operating losses it was lines such as this that were axed. Little account was taken of the fact that Embsay yard was shunted twice a day to move the quarried stone to where it was needed. Neither was any thought given to the loss of passengers travelling beyond Skipton to Bradford, Leeds and beyond. So it came as little surprise that the line from Ilkley to Skipton was axed with the last trains running on Saturday 20 March 1965.

The Preservation Era

The section of line from Ilkley to Embsay was quickly lifted leaving the line from Skipton to Grassington open for stone traffic from the local quarries. These were expected to close within a few years. However, a group of enthusiasts had other ideas and a meeting at Skipton Town Hall on 21 October 1968 resulted in the formation of the Embsay & Grassington Railway Society whose aim was to run steam trains to Grassington using Embsay as their base.

Only quick action, a sit-in at Embsay and help from the local MP stopped British Rail from dismantling the track from the quarry sidings through Embsay station to its junction with the Grassington line, allowing the society to rent the site at Embsay for storing rolling stock. Meanwhile Tilcon had purchased the quarry at Swinden, near Grassington, and were intending to send the stone out by train. With the Grassington line out of reach the society decided to concentrate its efforts on the abandoned Embsay to Bolton Abbey route.

By 1972 there were six small ex-industrial tank engines at Embsay and the early 1970s saw trains running from Embsay to Bow Bridge loop, close to the junction with the Grassington line. Unfortunately in 1974 BR banned these trains due to insurance liability and it was not until 1979 when a Light Railway Order was obtained that trains began running again. By the time rails were laid to Skibeden in 1982 the society had changed its name to the Embsay Steam Railway. In 1987 another half mile of track was opened to Holywell Halt and in April 1991 trains started running to Stoneacre Loop, some 2 miles from Embsay. Bolton Abbey was reached in 1997 with the first passenger train arriving on 26 October. Although the station is over a mile from the ruined abbey of the same name it attracts walkers and visitors to the railway, which is now 5 miles in length. The station at Bolton Abbey is a replica of the original Midland Railway wooden buildings and was built with help from Yorkshire Television's *Action Time* programme with McAlpine's completing the construction work free of charge.

With the railway open to Bolton Abbey its name was changed once more. It now trades under the title of the Embsay & Bolton Abbey Steam Railway. Trains run throughout the year. In winter a Sunday only service is operated while for the rest of the year trains run on a weekend, except in the main summer holiday period when a daily timetable operates. Special events feature heavily on the railway with *Thomas the Tank Engine* and *Santa* trains being particularly popular along with gala weekends aimed at the enthusiast market.

The E&BASR is renowned for its use of ex-industrial locomotives but this has not stopped ex-BR engines from being hired in from time to time. Visiting engines have included 'J72'

0-6-0T No.69027 *Joem*, 'J27' 0-6-0 No.65894, '4F' 0-6-0 No.4422, 'Jinty' 0-6-0T No.47279 and '64XX' 0-6-0PT No.6430. Mainline diesels to visit have included a Class 20, Class 24 and Class 31 while in 1999 a Class 107 diesel multiple unit arrived on the railway and operates off-peak services. The majority of passenger coaches in use are BR Mark I vehicles, most of which date from the 1950s and 1960s.

Left: In the embryonic days of operations at Embsay trains were only run between Bow Bridge, Embsay station and Skibeden. In the early 1980s we see *Slough Estates No.5*, a Hudswell Clarke 0-6-0ST of 1939, at the head of a rake of two Gresley teak coaches and a Southern Region utility van about to depart with one of these shuttle workings.

Opposite above: The E&BASR has hired in a number of steam locomotives over the years and one of the first was the NELPG's BR built 'J72' Class 0-6-0T No.69023 *Joem*. On 29 August 1988 the 'J27' is pictured drifting down the gradient from Skibeden loop with three BR Mark I coaches in tow. The use of an ex-NER design is quite appropriate for Embsay as NER locomotives worked into Skipton via Otley and Embsay.

Opposite below: An engine yet to enter regular traffic is the ex-WR diesel hydraulic 0-6-0 No.D9513 seen here between Bow Bridge loop and Embsay station on 14 July 1991. The engine is in NCB dark blue livery as No.38. Although the original two-tone green livery of this class was very attractive, as this locomotive spent more time as a NCB engine than on BR the livery is quite appropriate.

In 1993 Fowler-designed LMS Class '4F' 0-6-0 No.4422 was hired in for the summer season. Here we see No.4422 working up the gradient from Bow Bridge loop toward Embsay station on 1 May 1993. This type of locomotive is again quite fitting for the E&BASR as Skipton and Hellifield sheds were allocated members of the class in LMS and BR days and used them on the line through Embsay and Ilkley.

On 4 May 1963 the RCTS 'Dalesman' railtour was worked over what is now the E&BASR and here we see the preserved Gresley Class 'K4' 2-6-0 *The Great Marquess* storming through Bolton Abbey station. At this time the station was used to store withdrawn carriages. (Andrew Wilson Collection)

It is 26 October 1997 and the official re-opening special to Bolton Abbey station has just arrived and the two locomotives, Andrew Barclay 0-4-0ST No.22 and Hunslet 0-6-0T *Primrose No.*, are in the process of running round their train. As can be seen both locomotives were cleaned to perfection for the occasion.

Sunday 21 August 2005 finds Hugh Shipton's ex-GWR Class '6400' 0-6-0PT No.6430 leaving Bolton Abbey with the first train of the day. Although only rated as 2P No.6430 proved more than capable of handling the five-coach trains used by the E&BASR. Despite being a long way from ex-GWR territory the pannier tank looks at home in the Yorkshire Dales.

The E&BASR relies heavily on 0-6-0Ts to work its normal services and on 12 August 2002 *Monckton No.1*, a product of the Hunslet Works in Leeds and built in 1953, is pictured at Bolton Abbey station waiting to return to Embsay. At present only one platform is in use at this station but as time and finances allow the second platform will be restored.

Another 0-6-0T to visit the railway is the K&WVR's ex-LMS Class '3F Jinty' 0-6-0T No.47279 seen running out of Hambleton cutting into Bolton Abbey station on Sunday 7 September 2003. The 'Jinty' was a very popular addition to the E&BASR's fleet while on loan and has made further visits to Embsay.

The gradient of line from Bolton Abbey to Priors Lane is against the collar and so the railway always has its locomotives working chimney first out of Bolton Abbey. On 2 November 1997 Hunslet 0-6-0T *Primrose No.2* is seen working hard on the climb toward Priors Lane with some 150 tons on the drawbar, a stiff test of the steaming capacity of these moderately dimensioned engines.

During the 2005–06 winter the North Norfolk Railway's 'J15' Class 0-6-0 No.65462 was hired in by the railway and proved to be a very popular engine attracting a great deal of media attention. On sunny 10 December 2005 the diminutive 'J15' is seen working almost flat out with six coaches in tow as it passes the permanent-way depot at Priors Lane with a Santa Special.

Left: Monckton No.1 is seen heading away from Stoneacre Loop toward Priors Lane on a gloriously sunny 24 August 2003. When looking at views such of this it is hard to realise that the railway was originally a double track secondary mainline which saw 'Royal Scot' 4-6-0s and Gresley 'A3' 4-6-2s as well as '8F' 2-8-0 s and '9F' 2-10-0s, a far cry from the 0-6-0ST seen here.

Below: Priors Lane is the setting for this photograph of '6400' Class 0-6-0PT No.6430 on 21 August 2005. On most normal service days each locomotive works five round trips, some 50 miles a day, and tank engines are by far the most economical locomotives to use. Although the bigger tender engines have a certain glamour, the tank engines are a practical solution to work the railway's trains.

Above: 'J15' Class 0-6-0 No.65462 is pictured leaving Stoneacre Loop for Embsay with a Santa Special on 10 December 2005. The change in gradient after leaving the loop is very obvious in this view. The loop here was built halfway between Embsay and Bolton Abbey to increase the capacity of the line and as a result has no road access.

Right: Hunslet 0-6-0ST *Primrose No.2* (NCB No.S121) pounds through Holywell bridge under the A59 Skipton to Harrogate road on 3 May 1993 into Holywell Halt. The re-built bridge only just provides sufficient clearance for the BR Mark I coaches even though the track bed has been lowered, a distinct dip in the track here being clearly apparent.

To allow the restoration of rolling stock to be undertaken under cover a three-road shed was built on the Bolton Abbey side of the yard at Embsay. The newly built shed is seen here after the fan of sidings had been laid. The building to the left is the Dutch barn used to keep some of the railway's carriages under cover.

Stephen Middleton has his Stately Trains vintage coaches based on the E&BASR. Here on 16 October 2004 Peckett 0-4-0ST No.1483 is seen coupled to one ex-GNOS and two ex-GER six-wheel coaches in Embsay station. The station building is the original Midland Railway edifice while the waiting room was originally sited at Barmouth on the Cambrian section of BR.

Thomas the Tank Engine specials feature highly in the railway's programme of events each year. For a while the E&BASR had two engines turned out as *Thomas*, as seen here on 26 May 2002. In the foreground are No.140 and the newly converted *Dorothy* both in steam together. The railway hires out *Thomas* for themed events on other railways and the income this provides is an important way of increasing receipts.

This classic country station scene at Embsay taken on 26 May 2002 is the first day that *Monckton No.1* was in use after being restored following some twenty years out of use. The left-hand track heads towards Bow Bridge loop and the site of the old junction with the Grassington branch. One of the E&BASR's long-term aims is to reinstate the junction and run trains into the mainline station at Skipton.

Visiting Andrew Barclay 0-4-0ST No.2274 of 1949 from the Bowes Railway is seen at Bow Bridge loop on a demonstration freight working during the Harvest of Steam gala on 16 October 2004. The site of the junction with the Grassington branch is just to the left of this photograph.

NCB 0-6-0ST No.S134 *Wheldale* is pictured making good progress toward Embsay station after running round its train at Bow Bridge loop on 13 May 1990. The pristine saddle tank's maroon livery matches that of the restored BR Mark I stock used by the railway. *Wheldale* is at present out of traffic awaiting a general overhaul.

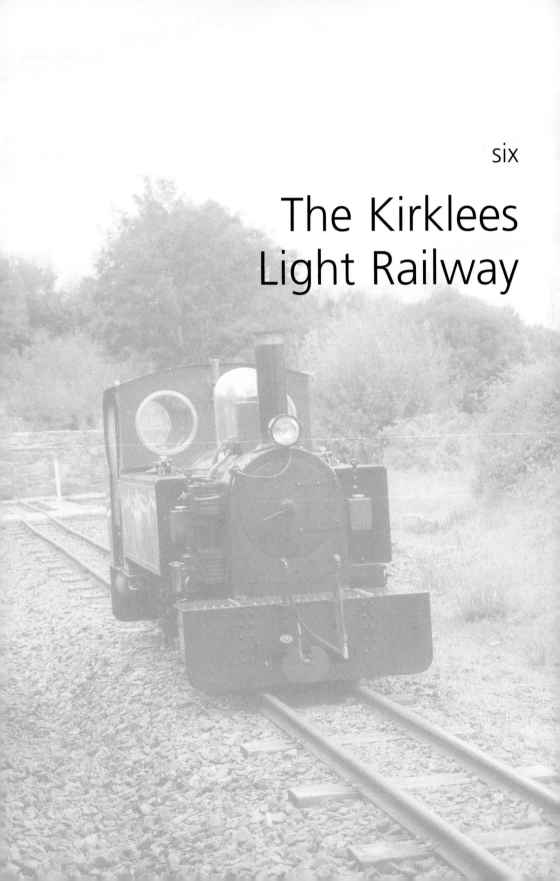

six

The Kirklees
Light Railway

Based at Clayton West in West Yorkshire this 15in gauge railway is built on the former trackbed of the erstwhile Lancashire & Yorkshire Railway branch line that opened in 1879. It left the mainline at Clayton West Junction and serviced several coalmines. At Skelmanthorpe it served the local pit and Park Mill Colliery which used its own internal tramway to bring coal to the standard-gauge line. Clayton West itself had a coal washing plant. There had been hopes to extend the line to Barnsley but the powers lapsed in 1899 and Clayton West was destined to remain the end of the line.

As with many branch lines a decline in its fortunes began in the early 1960s and despite the coal traffic still being heavy only a subsidy from the West Yorkshire County Council kept the line open. Passenger services ceased on 22 January 1983 and the branch closed the following October. Track lifting began three years later and Clayton West became a steel storage yard after being sold by BR.

This is where project engineer Brian Taylor enters the picture. Brian had previously built and operated a 10in gauge railway in Shibden Park near Halifax. Wanting a bigger challenge he had the vision of building a 15-inch gauge railway, along with all its locomotives and rolling stock, on the trackbed of the Clayton West branch. With the backing of the local council the project gained momentum. With a 125-year lease and an application for a Light Railway Order made in February 1989, a derelict land grant was made and work began designing and constructing the locomotives. The LRO was granted on 27 September 1991.

The old goods depot at Clayton West was converted into a workshop and engine shed. After the construction of a new engine and carriage shed the workshop now occupies the whole of the goods shed. The old station building was beyond economic repair and so was demolished and replaced by a purpose built station with living accommodation above.

The first section of the Kirklees Light Railway opened in October 1991 and ran for a mile from Clayton West to a new halt called Cuckoo's Nest. On Boxing Day 1992 the railway extended to Skelmanthorpe and four years later to Shelley. To reach the new terminus the line passes through Shelley Woodhouse tunnel which, at 511 yards in length, is the longest on any narrow-gauge railway in the country. A proposal for the future is the development of an interchange station at Shelley with the standard-gauge line from Huddersfield.

Having achieved his aim of building and operating his own railway Brian Taylor decided the time was right to put the Kirklees Light Railway up for sale. On 1 January 2006 Graham Hurd, whose intention is to raise the profile of the railway and improve the facilities at Clayton West, bought the railway for an undisclosed sum. There are also long-term plans to build more coaches, including one for disabled visitors.

Clayton West station on 8 August 2002 finds 2-6-2T *Fox*, built in 1987, at the head of a three-coach mid-train for Shelley. The new station buildings can be seen behind the train and the small size of the 15in-gauge line is emphasised by the people on the platform.

The stock shed at Clayton West is a large commodious building and one of its occupants on 8 August 2002 is 0-6-4T *Badger*, built in 1991. Each of the Kirklees Light Railway engines is painted in a different livery; *Badger* is seen in light green lined out in yellow. To the left of *Badger* is one of the shed's inspection pits.

In this February 1969 view of Clayton West looking towards Shelley the goods shed and signal box stand out in a bleak winter's scene. Today only the goods shed remains standing and this picture makes a very interesting comparison with the one below. What were line-side bushes in 1969 have grown and matured into handsome trees. (Kidderminster Railway Museum)

Running into Clayton West on 8 August 2002 with a train from Shelley 2-6-2T, *Fox* is framed by some of the tall broad-leafed trees that have grown along the line. *Fox* is running past the goods shed, seen above, which is just out of view to the left of this picture. *Fox* carries an attractive bright red livery lined out in yellow and black.

Like many steam railways the Kirklees Light Railway has a number of internal combustion locomotives to work maintenance or low season trains. Pictured at Shelley is *Jay*, a four-wheel diesel built in 1992. The names of the engines have been carefully chosen to reflect some of the wildlife passengers may see on a return journey to Shelley.

Having been turned at Shelley, *Fox* is ready to return to Clayton West. The ex-Lancashire & Yorkshire Huddersfield to Penistone line passes very close to here and plans have been mooted to build an interchange station with the standard-gauge line close to this spot.

Although built to a freelance design, *Fox* has more than a passing similarity to the Leek & Manifold Railway's tank engines. In the distance behind *Fox* is the Emley Moor television transmitter that dominates the countryside for miles around this part of West Yorkshire. *Fox* will shortly leave Shelley for the return run to Clayton West.

The Kirklees Light Railways possesses two articulated steam locomotives, *Owl* and *Hawk*. In the foreground is geared 4w-4wT *Owl* in yellow ochre livery with 0-4-4-0 *Hawk* behind in blue livery lined out in white and black. Both locomotives are powerful machines and are generally only used when traffic is heavy.

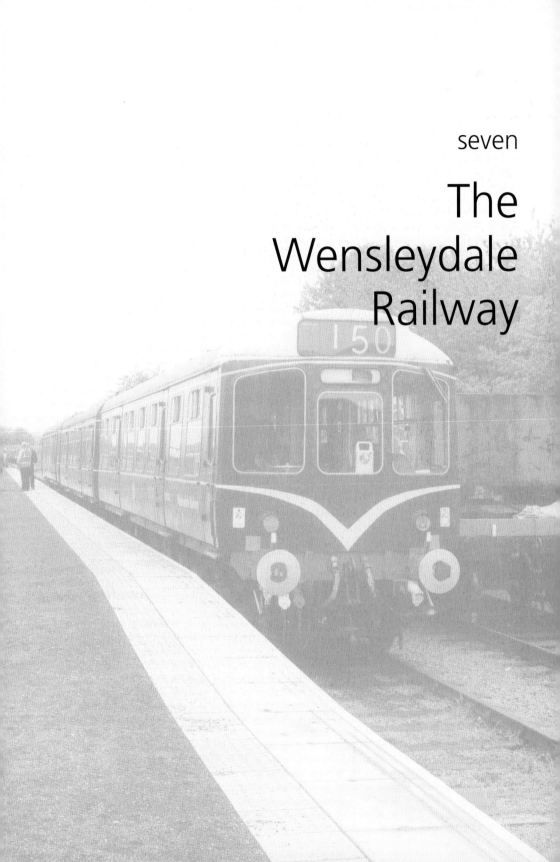

seven

The Wensleydale Railway

The Wensleydale Railway was built along the valley of the River Ure to link the railways east of the Pennines with those to the west. Constructed between 1847 and 1878 it linked Northallerton on the East Coast mainline to Hawes Junction, re-named Garsdale in 1933, on the Settle & Carlisle. At almost 40 miles in length it was one of the North Eastern Railway's more significant secondary lines of which the western section, between Hawes and Garsdale, was shared with the Midland Railway.

Construction of the first 7 miles from Northallerton to Bedale began in February 1847 and on 6 March 1848 the Northallerton to Leeming section opened. An extension to Leyburn was begun in February 1854 and opened to both passenger and goods traffic on 19 May 1856. Worked by the North Eastern Railway a service of four passenger trains a day, augmented to five on market days, was provided. On 8 August 1859 the independent Bedale & Leyburn Railway was amalgamated with the North Eastern Railway.

The construction of the Settle & Carlisle line with its branch from Hawes Junction to Hawes led the NER to extend its line further along the valley of the River Ure to meet the Midland Railway at Hawes. Trains began running between Askrigg and Hawes on 1 June 1878 and on 1 August goods workings were extended to Hawes Junction. The passenger services remained at four or five trains a day and by 1868 Leyburn was selling 14,000 tickets a year, a figure that was to peak at 26,000 in 1880. The Midland's 5¾ miles of track were never to carry the passenger traffic enjoyed by the rest of the branch. In 1879, the line's first full year of operation, only 6,845 tickets were sold, a figure that peaked at 9,193 in 1891.

From 1874 the Fletcher BTP 0-4-4Ts started working the line and continued until the 1920s when they were replaced by Worsdell 'A' Class 2-4-2Ts. Goods work was handled by 0-6-0s, although from time to time 0-6-2Ts were used. Three engine sheds, at Leyburn, Northallerton and Hawes, were built to service the engines working, the line allowing crews to be based at both Northallerton and Hawes.

The goods traffic handled on the line was predominantly agricultural in nature. Coal and general merchandise was brought in and, apart from limestone, local farms generated the bulk of the outgoing traffic. In 1868 Leyburn handled 5,044 sheep, a figure that rose to 21,509 in 1891 when 10,699 cattle were also dealt with. By 1894 milk was being despatched via Northallerton to Newcastle, Middlesbrough, Hull and Leeds and within five years it was also going to Bradford, Halifax and other West Riding towns and later to Liverpool and Finsbury Park, London. In 1899 27,000 gallons were despatched by rail. In 1905 this rose to 426,000 gallons and the following year to 502,000 gallons. As a result there was at least one milk train each day, including Sundays. In 1932 centralised milk depots were set up at Leyburn and Appleby which used road tankers to bring the milk direct from the local farms. This hit the railway very hard and quickly the once extensive milk workings were reduced to just one a day.

The limestone quarries at Redmire, Wensley and Leyburn were significant sources of traffic with limestone being required in large quantities as flux in the iron and steel works on Teeside. Normally one train a day catered for this traffic but when demand was heavy extra workings were provided. Demand for limestone varied; in 1875 28,700 tons were despatched from Leyburn, 11,000 tons in 1920 and 44,000 tons in 1927. Production at the Redmire quarry quickly rose from 11,000 tons in 1921 to over 33,000 tons in 1923 but then fluctuated in response to the demand. Similarly the quarry at Wensley peaked at 47,000 tons in 1935 before beginning a gradual decline.

In 1923 the Wensleydale line as far as Hawes passed to the LNER and to the LMS as far as Hawes Junction. The 1920s brought about the withdrawal of the BTP 0-4-4Ts and their replacement by Class 'A', (F8), 2-4-2Ts. These in turn were replaced by 'G5' Class 0-4-4Ts the first of which arrived at Northallerton in 1929. In 1930 Northallerton received 'D17/1' 4-4-0 No.1636 to work the milk train to and from Hawes. At Hawes first a 0-6-0 was allocated and then a 'F8' and finally on 30 May 1935 a 'G5' arrived.

The eclipse of the sun on 29 June 1927 brought a considerable amount of special traffic to Leyburn as this was the first total eclipse since 1724. The moon was due to obscure the sun at 6.24a.m. and so all the excursions had very early starts and came from King's Cross, Colchester, Dewsbury, Hull, Leeds, Norwich, Nottingham and Scarborough. Special water tenders and extra gas-tanks wagons were brought to Leyburn to service the excursion stock before their return journeys. The eclipse itself was a bit of a disappointment as the sky clouded over. The best conditions were found a little further south at Giggleswick. In 1936, static camping coaches were put in at Wensley, Aysgarth and Askrigg. The three coaches were maintained up to and including 1939 but were not reinstated after 1945.

The outbreak of war on September 3 1939 hardly touched the Wensleydale line although its value as a trans-Pennine route was not forgotten. The passenger service remained, worked by two trains which provided four return trips. What did affect the eastern end of the line, however, was the establishment of a RAF Bomber Command airfield at Leeming. This brought with it considerable extra traffic as munitions, stores and servicemen and women were sent to and from Leeming.

In the immediate post-war period there was little change on the line. Despite the nationalisation of the railways in 1948 the operation of the passenger and goods trains continued much as they had done in the 1930s. However, the changed social and economic conditions made it hard for lines such as that through Wensleydale to cover their costs. The only assured goods traffic was from the quarries and their output was declining. The biggest problem was the lack of passengers. The growth of motor transport completely changed the nature of the milk traffic in the 1930s and the more convenient motorbus had lured many passengers with its village centre to village centre service. The 'G5' 0-4-4Ts were still in charge of the passenger trains. The goods turns were in the hands of 'J21' and 'J25' 0-6-0s. One change was the use of 'D20' 4-4-0s allocated to Northallerton on the passenger services.

In 1953 it was announced that the passenger service between Northallerton and Garsdale would be withdrawn despite its value as a social service in severe winters when many of the roads became impassable. British Railways claimed that the passenger service was losing £14,500 a year and was only used by 2 per cent of the dales population. Despite local opposition closure was approved and the final day was set for 29 March 1954. As there was insufficient time to set up a replacement bus service actual closure came on 26 April with the last trains running on Saturday 24 April when 'J21' No.65038 worked the 9.30a.m. Northallerton to Hawes while 'D20' No. 62347 was in charge of the 1.33p.m. departure. No.65038 then took the 4.10p.m. train to Hawes and No.62347 worked the final departure from Northallerton at 9.05p.m. One last passenger train ran next day when 'G5' No.67345 worked the Sunday Northallerton to Leyburn working. The only trains to now run over the whole length of the line were the pick-up freights.

The Arctic winters of 1962 and 1963 briefly brought the line back into the limelight. In January 1962 blizzard conditions blocked most roads through the dale and an emergency passenger train was hastily put into service but only after snowplough fitted Ivatt 2-6-0 No. 46475 cleared the line. This allowed 'K1' 2-6-0 No.62044 and J21 0-6-0 No.65044 to maintain a skeleton service until the roads were re-opened. The following year's even worse winter again found the railway able to serve the isolated communities until the roads were cleared.

With the Beeching report published it was only a matter of time before the goods services were pruned back. This happened on 27 April 1964 when the line was closed between Redmire and Hawes. By 1967 only Leyburn, Bedale and Redmire remained open handling coal, oil, sugar beet and limestone traffic. Further rationalisation occurred in 1983 when the line to Leyburn was reduced to one train operation allowing the closure of all the signal-boxes except Bedale. Redmire quarry remained rail linked into the 1990s when the line was mothballed and effectively closed.

The reprieve of the Settle-Carlisle line in 1989 prompted the formation of the Wensleydale Railway Association in 1990 whose aim was to bring back passenger services to the surviving 22-mile track. A long-term goal was restoring the full 40-mile route of the original Wensleydale railway. In 1995 the privatisation of British Rail led the WRA to take a more active part in ensuring the return of rail services to Wensleydale. In 2000 the WRA formed a company, Wensleydale Railway plc, which launched a share offer to raise funds for the development and operation of the line. More than £2 million was raised. Three years later a ninety-nine-year lease was agreed with Network Rail for the 22 miles of track between Northallerton and Redmire, allowing these stations to be re-opened. Bedale and Redmire stations re-opened on 1 August 2004 and Finghall on 23 December 2004. Passenger services using diesel multiple units began on 4 July, 2003 between Leeming Bar and Leyburn (12 miles). In 2004 train services were extended by nearly 5 miles to Redmire and three more stations were re-opened: Bedale, Finghall and Redmire. A second share offer was also launched to raise further money. Substantial infrastructure works undertaken in 2005 allowed the raising of speed limits, now 25mph for dmu trains and 15mph for freight, and the controlled introduction of some loco-hauled diesel services using Class 31 No.31166 and Class 37 Nos 37003 and 37198 during August.

For two weeks in September 2005 the Parry 50 people mover railcar ran trials between Leeming Bar and Springwells Lane, just outside Northallerton, linking up with a bus service to the town centre. The patronage was such as to show a significant public demand for re-opening the line through to Northallerton, and this is now a goal of the Wensleydale Railway. The railway was again in the news on 19 August 2006 when steam retuned to the line in the shape of Mansell ' King Arthur' Class 2-6-0 No.30777 *Sir Lamiel* which was in charge of a Railway Touring Co. special, running from Northallerton over the whole length of the re-opened line.

The first total eclipse of the sun seen in England since 1724 took place on 29 June 1927. This event generated considerable public interest and special trains were run to the north of England to view the spectacle. One of the many excursions is pictured here running into Leyburn station behind 4-4-0 No.711 and 4-6-0 No.1372. (H.C. Casserley)

The dairy at Leyburn generated enough traffic to warrant the allocation of a shunter there. In February 1954 we see Class 'Y3' Sentinel No.68182 waiting the arrival of the next up train to which it will attach these four milk tankers. (J.W. Armstrong Trust)

Ex-NER Class 'G5' 0-4-4T No.67294 runs into Jervaulx station with a local working *circa* 1954. The station here served the ruined Jervaulx Abbey and attracted trainloads of visitors at weekends and bank holidays, despite the fact that the abbey was some 3 miles south of the station which it purported to serve. (J.W. Armstrong Trust)

The quarry at Redmire was a very important source of traffic for the Wensleydale Railway. Here we see Peppercorn Class 'K1' 2-6-0 No.62045 shunting at Redmire. Although the line was truncated west of Redmire, the quarry traffic ensured the line to Northallerton was maintained in a condition able to handle these heavy workings. (Neville Stead Collection)

Class 60 Type '5' Co-Co diesel No.60049 is pictured at the head of a train of high capacity hopper wagons near Leeming Bar. The construction industry's insatiable appetite for hardcore ensures that most rail-connected quarries see a healthy number of trains such as this one. (Neville Stead Collection)

The Wensleydale Railway has its headquarters at Leeming Bar and here on Saturday, 13 May 2006 we see three of the railway's diesel locomotives. On the left are Class 31 A1A-A1As Nos D5611 and D5584 alongside an unidentified Class 37 undergoing restoration.

The passenger service between Leeming Bar and Redmire is operated by heritage diesel multiple units. On 13 May 2006 three-car Birmingham Railway & Carriage Works Class 110 unit was working the public trains. The Saturday timetable comprised three round trips.

An almost deserted Leeming Bar station on 13 May 2006. Class 37 No.37003 is parked in the loop along with the railway's brakedown crane. Across the level crossing at the end of the platform the line heads east toward the East Coast mainline at Northallerton.

Right: The Wensleydale Railway's BRCW Class 110 diesel multiple units runs into Leeming Bar station with the return working of the first train of the day from Redmire. The road in the background is the A1 under which the railway tunnels on the way to Leyburn.

Below: As with many new heritage railway schemes the Wensleydale Railway is chronically short of covered accommodation for its rolling stock and here we see some of the railway's coaches, dmus and goods wagons parked at Leeming Bar in the shadow of the A1. Unfortunately this leaves the railway open to attacks by so-called graffiti artists who do no end of damage to restored items.

A view of some more of the Wensleydale Railway's rolling stock stored at Leeming Bar station yard. In the foreground is ex-Southern Region DMBSO No.9010, which still retains it third-rail collector shoes, and behind is an ex-Regional Railways Class 101 diesel multiple unit undergoing restoration.

The problem that the railway has with restoring its stock in the open is apparent in this view of the Class 101 diesel multiple unit. The Regional Railways livery has been defaced by the mindless actions of the 'graffiti artists' who seem to have little or no appreciation of the hard work entailed in the restoration of any item of rolling stock.

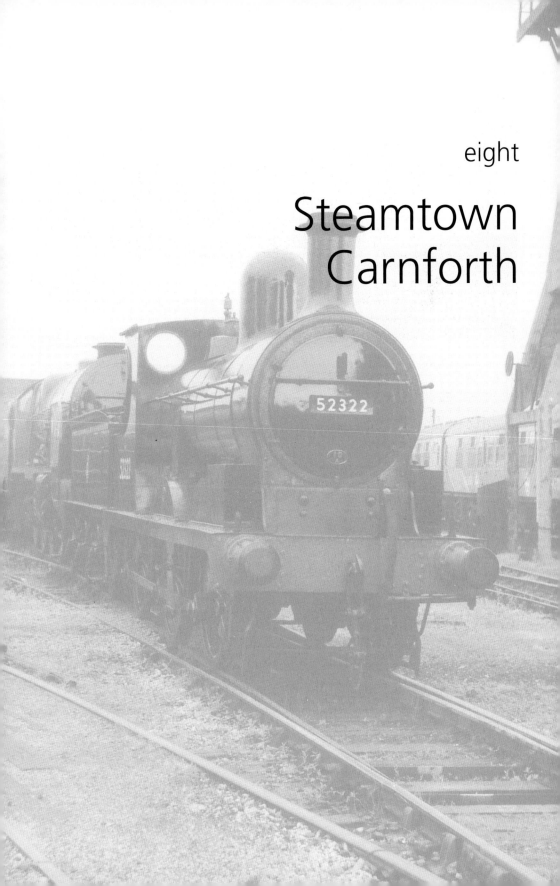

eight

Steamtown Carnforth

When Carnforth engine shed was closed by BR in summer 1968 it became the focus of a projected steam museum under the leadership of Dr Peter Beet. The site was leased from BR to provide a home for a number of preserved steam locomotives ranging from small industrial 0-4-0STs to 'Black Fives' and eventually a French and German Pacific.

The area leased covered nearly 70 acres and in addition to the running shed, workshops and offices, included a coaling tower, an ash disposal plant, a 70ft turntable, water columns and a carriage and wagon works. A demonstration line was developed within the site – the Crag Bank shuttle – which allowed rides to be taken from one end of the site to the other, along with a shorter miniature railway. In the early 1970s Carnforth became the base for steam locomotives running over BR tracks, particularly those working the 'Cumbrian Mountain Express' to Hellifield and then over the Settle & Carlisle.

Unfortunately, by the late 1980s the condition of the engine shed was giving rise to alarm as the concrete used in its construction began to degrade. Health and safety concerns eventually led to the closure of Steamtown to the public. However, the site has now become the base of the West Coast Railway Co. which supplies coaches for railtours and is also the home of ex-LMS '8F' 2-8-0 No.48151 and ex-GWR 'Hall' Class 4-6-0 No.5972 *Oulton Hall*, both of which are certificated to run on the mainline. No.5972 has gained fame as *Hogwarts Castle* and in red livery has starred in the popular *Harry Potter* films. Two other mainline locomotives are currently being overhauled at Carnforth and these are 'Royal Scot' No.46115 *Scots Guardsman* and 'Jubilee' No.45699 *Galatea*. The workshops at Carnforth also specialise in the heavy overhauls of steam locomotives as well as carriage restoration.

The heyday of Steamtown Carnforth, when it was an active depot servicing locomotives used on mainline excursions, on 1 May 1976. Three locomotives are being made ready for their trains, ex-LNWR 2-4-0 No.790 *Hardwicke*, Thompson 'B1' Class 4-6-0 No.1306 *Mayflower* and LNER Class 'A3' Pacific No.4472 *Flying Scotsman*. In the background is the depot's coaling plant and to the right the ash plant.

Carnforth was one of British Railway's last operational steam depots and when taken over retained all its servicing features. Here Thompson 'B1' Class 4-6-0 No.1306 *Mayflower* is seen on the shed's turntable on 5 June 1971. No.1306 is now based on the Nene Valley Railway after spending a period at Loughborough on the Great Central Railway.

A number of preserved Stanier 'Black Five' 4-6-0s were initially based at Carnforth and here we see two of them, Nos 45407 and 44871. No.45407 is now owned by Ian Riley and nominally based at Bury from where it works regularly on the mainline. No.44871 is out of traffic at the East Lancashire Railway waiting its turn to be overhauled.

Above: 'Black Five' 4-6-0 No.45407 is pictured at Carnforth on 5 June 1971 when it was painted in reddish-brown Furness Railway livery with the tender lettered FR. A novel idea at the time the livery ill-suited the locomotive and it was soon repainted into an authentic lined out black British Railways livery.

Above: A number of ex-Barry scrapyard engines were brought to Carnforth for storage. On 26 May 1974 re-built 'Merchant Navy' Pacific No.35005 *Canadian Pacific* is pictured at the back of the shed building. *Canadian Pacific* is now based on the Mid-Hants Railway in Hampshire and has been used on a number of highly enterprising mainline trips.

Right: Ex-Great Western Railway '5600' Class 0-6-2T No.5643 is seen stored inside the shed on 26 May 1974. No.5643 was bought for use on the Lakeside & Haverthwaite Railway and at the time of writing is nearing the completion of its heavy overhaul, some thirty-two years after this picture was taken, at Haverthwaite.

Opposite below: As well as being home to a number of mainline locomotives, Carnforth also housed a large number of industrial tank engines. Two of the resident Andrew Barclay 0-4-0STs are seen here, *John Howe* and *Cooke & Nuttall No.1*. The small 0-4-0STs were used on the Crag Bank shuttles on off-peak days when it was uneconomical to steam an ex-mainline locomotive. *John Howe* is now at the Ribble Steam Railway.

The National Railway Museum's Midland Railway 'Compound' 4-4-0 No.1000 was restored to steam and used on a number of mainline workings. Here it is seen at Carnforth in the company of ex-Great Western Railway 'Modified Hall' Class 4-6-0 No.6960 *Raveningham Hall*. No.1000 is now back at York while No.6960 is based on the Gloucestershire & Warwickshire Railway.

Dr Beet's French pacific No.231 K22 is pictured in steam on Carnforth's ash road behind No.4472 *Flying Scotsman*. Both No.231 K22 and German Railway Pacific No.012 104-8 have been returned to the European mainland and are now on display in Switzerland.

The first British Railways Standard locomotive to be built, No.70000 *Britannia*, is pictured on 29 March 1991. After first being returned to steam on the Severn Valley Railway, *Britannia* was eventually overhauled to mainline standards where the work was completed at Carnforth. After this picture was taken No.70000 was used on a number of very successful mainline excursions.

Without a doubt the most widely travelled Gresley Class 'A3' Pacific is No.4472 *Flying Scotsman* seen here in steam against the backdrop of Carnforth's coaling plant. *Flying Scotsman* is now owned by the National Railway Museum where it has been used on the museum's mainline excursions between York and Scarborough but is at present in the throws of a general overhaul.

Although not seen at Carnforth, the re-built 'Royal Scot' Class 4-6-0 No.6115 *Scots Guardsman* is at present at Carnforth where it is being re-built to mainline standards. The three-cylinder 4-6-0 is pictured at one of its previous homes, the Dinting Railway Centre. Since Steamtown was closed to the public it has become a maintenance and overhaul centre for the West Coast Railway Co.

A long-term Carnforth resident was maroon-liveried Ivatt Class '2MT' 2-6-0 No.46441 seen here running into Skipton with a working from Carnforth on 24 July 1993. No.46441 requires another heavy overhaul before it can steam again and is at present located at the Ribble Railway Centre in Preston.

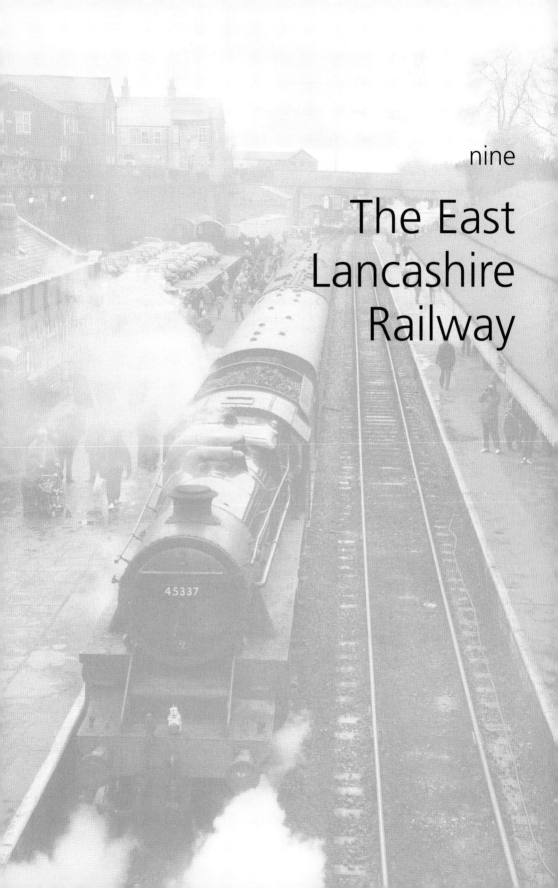

nine

The East
Lancashire
Railway

Authorised by Parliament on 24 July 1846 the East Lancashire Railway took only twenty-six months to construct. From Radcliffe Bridge the line climbed at 1 in 96 crossing and re-crossing the River Irwell, clinging to hillside ledges and plunging through steep cuttings. Between Clifton Bridge and Stubbins Junction the gradient eased to 1 in 132 while the climb to Rawtenstall lessened to 1 in 182. To reach Bacup, however, the climb stiffened to 1 in 71. Tunnels were bored at Bury, Brooksbottom, Nuttal and at Newchurch, Nos 1 and 2. Between Clifton Junction and Ramsbottom the line crossed the River Irwell no less than twelve times.

On 26 September 1846, at precisely 12.35p.m., the inaugural train departed from Manchester (Victoria). Three days later the public service began with fourteen trains running between Manchester and Bury, five of them running through to Rawtenstall. Intermediate stations were provided at Radcliffe Bridge, Summerseat and Ramsbottom but it was to be 1853 before they were all open to traffic. Bury station was built in a cutting and a small two-road goods shed was provided at Castlecroft along with a small engine shed to the south of the station. The line to Bacup was not ready for use until 1 October 1851 and the branch to Holcombe Brook was opened on 6 November 1882. Early motive power comprised a collection of 2-2-2, 2-4-0, 0-4-2, 0-4-0 and 0-6-0 engines built by a variety of contractors while passengers were carried in four-wheel and six-wheel coaches. By 1849 the level of service comprised no less than twenty-two return trains each weekday with five on a Sunday.

On 13 August 1859 the East Lancashire Railway merged with the Lancashire & Yorkshire Railway but it was not until 1875, with the appointment of William Barton Wright as Locomotive Superintendent, that a start was made to replace many of the archaic locomotives in use. Eventually his designs of 0-6-0s, 0-4-4Ts, 4-4-0s and 0-6-2Ts became commonplace. In 1876 a new and enlarged engine shed was opened at Bury and six years later a new shed was built at Bacup.

Such was the success of the East Lancashire Railway that in 1880 almost 100 trains were passing through Bury each weekday. Goods traffic was buoyant with coal being delivered to the cotton mills and train loads of finished goods taken away. To accommodate this level of traffic Bury Bolton Street station was rebuilt and enlarged.

The resignation of Barton Wright in 1886 led to the appointment of John Aspinall and his 2-4-2Ts and 0-6-0s were to dominate the lines through the Irwell Valley well into the late 1950s. In 1910, Bury Bolton Street station saw no less than 100 departures and the equivalent arrivals each weekday. Forty-four trains were despatched to Manchester Victoria, twenty-two to Holcombe Brook, sixteen to Bacup, fifteen to Accrington and three to Ramsbottom. Sundays saw a reduced service of thirty-seven departures.

On 29 July 1913 the Holcombe Brook branch was electrified and such was the success of this venture that the Manchester to Bury line was also electrified at 1,200-volts DC picking up from conductor rails. The new electric service provided trains every twenty minutes but during the rush hours departures were timed at ten-minute intervals.

By 1923 Bury shed was home to just over fifty engines while Bacup housed another twenty. These were made up of 0-6-0s, 0-6-0STs, 2-4-2Ts and 0-8-0s. The 2-4-2Ts handled the passenger traffic on the non-electrified lines while the 0-6-0STs shunted the various yards in the district leaving the 0-6-0s and 0-8-0s to handle the heavy goods workings. Gradually standard LMS designs such as the 2P 4-4-0s, 4F 0-6-0s and 7F 0-8-0s began to replace some of the older L&YR designs. These were then followed by 2-6-2Ts, 2-6-4Ts and 0-6-0Ts. The Second World War brought a significant drop in the number of passenger trains but the increased number of freight trains more than compensated for this.

A feature of the summer timetables, both before and after the war, were the Wakes Week holiday trains. The mills and factories in each town would all close down for a week's holiday. This created a huge number of unbalanced workings to holiday resorts such as Blackpool, Torquay, Skegness, Llandudno, Southport and Brighton. The Blackpool illuminations would also see large numbers of weekend excursions run from the East Lancashire towns to the west coast.

In 1952 Bury Bolton Street station was rebuilt after a fire in 1947 severely damaged the buildings. In the same year the passenger service to Holcombe Brook was withdrawn. Early in 1956 diesel multiple-units replaced the push-pull train between Bury and Bacup and in 1959 new electric trains replaced the old L&YR units. The 1960s saw the closure of the line from Rawtenstall to Bacup with Bury engine shed becoming redundant in 1965. At the beginning of 1968 Bury still had services to Manchester, Rawtenstall, Rochdale and Bolton but by 1971 only the Manchester to Rawtenstall trains remained. Finally in 1980 the electric service was withdrawn and the goods trains were stopped on 5 December, effectively bringing the curtain down on train services in the Irwell Valley. The East Lancashire Railway Preservation Society and local councils, however, had other ideas which were to see the East Lancashire Railway rise phoenix-like from the weed-strewn trackbeds of the Irwell Valley.

The Preservation Era

The East Lancashire Railway Society came into being in 1968 with the aim of preserving the Stubbins to Helmshore line as far as Grane Bridge. Despite raising funds and acquiring rolling stock the scheme foundered and in June 1971 an alternative site was sought. Eventually the goods shed at Castlecroft, Bury, was identified as a possible base and in 1972 a one-year lease was obtained allowing the society's stock to be transferred. When the last passenger train ran over the Bury to Rawtenstall line on 3 June 1971 the society entered negotiations with BR to operate a weekend steam service over the line.

In August 1973 BR made it clear that their policy was not to permit a preservation society to share its lines. Undaunted, the Castlecroft base was developed with more visitor amenities and a short demonstration line was laid. However, the catalyst to the development of the present East Lancashire Railway was the running of the last electric train between Bury Bolton Street and Manchester on 14 March 1980. BR was persuaded not to lift the track as negotiations continued between with the society, BR and the Greater Manchester Council. The breakthrough came on 9 November 1983 when the Greater Manchester Council learnt that it had been granted a derelict lands grant that could be used to develop the Bury to Rawtenstall railway as a tourist attraction.

After a number of false starts a Light Railway Order was gained in February 1986 which allowed the railway to run public trains between Bury Bolton Street and Rawtenstall. The official re-opening between Bury and Ramsbottom came on Saturday 25 July 1987. During the following years a great deal of work was put into restoring the infrastructure and acquiring locomotives and carriages. The Ramsbottom to Rawtenstall section of line required the re-building of four bridges and much attention to the track. Such was the amount of work needed that trains did not start running to Rawtenstall until April 1991. A new station building was opened at Rawtenstall in April 1992.

Locomotive and carriage facilities were developed at Bury and at Buckley Wells a carriage restoration shed was built on the site of the old coal yard. The society has also acquired the old electric car shops which were the original East Lancashire Railway workshops of 1846. These have been turned into a comprehensive locomotive works where the heaviest of overhauls can be undertaken.

As with many preservation schemes, the first locomotives to arrive on site were ex-industrial engines. The first ex-mainline engine to arrive was ex-LMS 'Jinty' 0-6-0T No.47298 in August 1988 and was followed a year later by Standard '4MT' 2-6-0 No.76079. Although these two engines have since departed elsewhere other locomotives such as ex-LMS 'Crab' 2-6-0 No.42765 and 'Black Five' 4-6-0 No.45337 have arrived. The railway has also been fortunate to be able to hire in ex-mainline locomotives such as 'Battle of Britain' Pacific No.34072 *257 Squadron* for extended visits. With the opening of the locomotive works newly overhauled locomotives such as 'Princess Royal' Pacific No.6201 *Princess Elizabeth*, BR Standard '8P' 4-6-2 No.71000 *Duke of Gloucester* and 'Battle of Britain' Pacific No.34067 *Tangmere* have been run in on East Lancashire Railway trains.

The railway has also built up a comprehensive collection of ex-mainline diesels with examples of three of the Western Region's diesel hydraulics: 'Warship' No.D832 *Onslaught*, 'Western' No.D1041 *Western Prince* and 'Hymek' No.D7076. Other diesel classes represented include 24, 25, 40 and 45. The railway also has a number of diesel multiple-units as well as shunting engines. Coaching stock is made up of BR Mark I stock.

Rawtenstall station on a wet 8 October 1964 illustrates the original ELR through station between Bury and Bacup. The main station buildings are to the left on the line to Bacup while the shelter and canopy offer some protection from the elements for passengers waiting to travel down to Bury and Manchester. (Roger Carpenter Collection)

Before services could re-start between Ramsbottom and Rawtenstall the preservation society, with financial support from the local councils, built a new station at Rawtenstall. Seen on 15 February 1998 the new terminal station mirrors the architectural style of the original ELR.

The frontage of the old station at Rawtenstall, photographed on 8 October 1964, has seen better days but does show the layout of the footbridge and goods yard, still cobbled, with its weigh house. Today the new station and its car park share the site with a supermarket, emphasising the considerable changes in society over the last fifty years. (Roger Carpenter Collection)

The level crossing at Rawtenstall remains extant and a brick-built signal box now stands guardian over the railway and road. The station is out of sight behind the mill buildings in the centre background. The relative lack of cars in this picture taken on 8 October 1964 is another sign of how this part of East Lancashire has evolved over the intervening half century. (Roger Carpenter Collection)

Since re-opening, the East Lancashire Railway has had a varied fleet of steam locomotives operate its services, many of which have been hired in. On 15 February 1998 Mrs Betty Beet's Ivatt '2MT' Class 2-6-0 No.46441 is about to run round its train in readiness to return to Bury Bolton Street station. No.46441 has been beautifully painted in LMR lined maroon, a livery it never carried in BR service.

The NRM's Stanier 'Princess Coronation' Class Pacific No.46229 *Duchess of Hamilton* is pictured at Ramsbottom station on 21 February 1998. No.46229 was nearing the end of its boiler certificate and had temporarily been re-painted into BR lined green livery for the ELR's late winter gala. After the event *Duchess of Hamilton* was returned to its previous LMR lined maroon livery.

The East Lancashire Railway is in the fortunate position of being able to run locomotives from all four pre-nationalisation railway companies, including the wide ex-GWR outside cylinder classes. On 14 November 1992 BR built '7800' Class 4-6-0 No.7828 *Odney Manor* pilots GWR 'Castle' Class 4-6-0 No.5029 *Nunney Castle* as they burst out of Bury tunnel past the ELR's original engine shed.

Another ex-BR locomotive to see use on the ELR is Gresley 'A4' Pacific No.60007 *Sir Nigel Gresley*, seen at Bury Bolton Street station on 14 November 1992. No.60007 is in BR lined blue livery which suits the elegant lines of the 'A4' well. Although carrying the 'Tyne-Tees Pullman' headboard the coaches are all BR Mark I stock in maroon livery.

With the opening of the branch to Heywood the ELR is able to offer two very different journeys to its customers. On 29 February 2004 the NELPG's ex-NER 'J27' Class 0-6-0 No.65894 brings a shuttle working from Heywood into Bury Bolton Street station. Although not obvious from this angle the station here is in a deep cutting with the ticket office built over the running lines at street level.

A number of diesel multiple-units are based on the ELR and used during themed diesel events and at galas to shuttle passengers to and from the railway's main engine shed and Bury Bolton Street station. Despite having less appeal than the steam-hauled trains the dmus are still maintained and presented in pristine condition.

Often locomotives from other preserved railways are sent to Ian Riley's Works for overhaul and are used on ELR services either before entering the workshops or as running-in trips. On 29 February 2004 the North Norfolk Railways ex-LNER 'B12' Class 4-6-0 No.61572 is pictured at Bury Bolton Street during the ELR's gala before going into the works. No.61572 is the only extant inside cylinder 4-6-0 in this country.

The ELR does not only hire in large and powerful locomotives, as this picture of ex-GWR '14XX' Class 0-4-2T No.1450 shows. Built to work the GWR's auto-trains on rural branches these little tank engines could punch above their weight. Restored to BR unlined black livery No.1450 is pictured at a wet Bury Bolton Street station on 31 January 1999.

Pictured outside the works and engine shed at Buckley Wells on 31 January 1999 are three of the ELR's preserved mainline diesels. Class 24 No.D5054 is nearest the camera with 'Warship' No.D832 *Onslaught* and Class 40 No.D345 behind. Apart from *Onslaught*, which is in black livery, the Class 24 and Class 40 are in authentic BR liveries, D5054 in green and the Class 40 in corporate blue.

The ELR is one of the few preserved railways able to re-create an authentic engine shed scene. On 19 August 1993 Buckley Wells yard is home to, from left to right, BR '4MT' Class 2-6-0 No.76079, ex-GWR '28XX' 2-8-0 No.3822, an ex-London Transport 0-6-0PT, a BR '08' diesel shunter and BR '9F' 2-10-0 No.92203 *Black Prince*.

Ian Riley's works have established a reputation for overhauling steam locomotives to the highest possible standard. Inside the works is Bulleid 'Battle of Britain' Pacific No.34067 *Tangmere* in the process of being restored from scrapyard condition to mainline certification. Since it was returned to steam *Tangmere* has become one of the most reliable locomotives operating on the mainline.

Most steam locomotives arrive on the ELR by road. Here we see what appears to be ex-LMS 'Jubilee' 4-6-0 No.5552 *Silver Jubilee* about to be unloaded at Bury on 16 August 1994. This is, in fact, sister 'Jubilee' No.45593 *Kolhapur* masquerading as *Silver Jubilee*.

The NELPG's Peppercorn 'K1' 2-6-0 No.62005 is seen without its wheels outside Ian Riley's workshops. The 'K1' was receiving a 'bottom overhaul' to its wheels, axleboxes and motion before heading north to Fort William where it was booked to work the summer season of 'Jacobite' steam trains to Mallaig.

Although a relatively latecomer to the rank of the preserved railways in England the East Lancashire Railway is able to operate the heaviest of ex-mainline locomotives such as 'A4' Class 4-6-2 No.60007 *Sir Nigel Gresley* seen here at Bury Bolton Street station on a dismal 31 January 1999. No.60007 is normally based on the NYMR when not running on the national network.

Newly restored BR Standard '4MT' Class 2-6-4T No.80136 is pictured at Bury Bolton Street station with a local working to Rawtenstall on 31 January 1999. Another of these handsome tank engines, No.80097, is based on the railway and nearing the end of a major restoration project from scrapyard condition and will soon be joining the ELR's operational fleet.

On 21 February 1998 BR Standard Class '4MT' 4-6-0 No.75014 arrives at Ramsbottom with a seven-coach train from Rawtenstall. No.75014 is now based on the Paignton & Dartmouth Steam Railway in south Devon.

A last look at the East Lancashire Railway sees the railway's Hughes/Fowler 'Crab' 2-6-0 No.42765 leaving Bury on 25 February 1995. This particular locomotive was the mainstay of the ELR's steam service for ten years and is now out of traffic awaiting a full mechanical and boiler overhaul. The 'Crabs' were regular performers over this line in both LMS and BR days making the use of No.42765 one of the most authentic on the ELR.

ten

The West Lancashire Light Railway

The origins of the West Lancashire Light Railway at Hesketh Bank date back to 1967 when a group of school friends set about creating their own narrow-gauge railway. Behind the back garden of Jonathan Whitehead's home was an old clay pit owned by his relatives and it is here that a 2ft-gauge railway has been built. Initially using second-hand materials, 150 yards of track were laid in the autumn of 1967. The first locomotive, a Ruston & Hornsby 13hp diesel named *Clwyd*, arrived in April 1968 and was used to pull a home-made four-wheel coach for rides.

In 1969 the first steam locomotive, an ex-Dinorwic Quarry Hunslet 0-4-0ST *Irish Mail*, arrived, albeit without a boiler. By 1970 there were 370 yards of track and in 1980 *Irish Mail* returned to steam. Since then the railway has not looked back as covered accommodation for the stock and a running shed were built. Such have been the developments that the railway now has a gift shop and can provide light refreshments for visitors. There are at the time of writing nine steam engines based on the railway and twenty-two four-wheel industrial diesels, but many of these are long-term restoration projects.

The running line is now some 430 yards long and there are two stations, Willow Tree Halt and Delph. At the latter there is a platform and run round loop. There is space for a further extension of 200 yards but as this would include a 1 in 40 bank all the stock would require fitting with continuous brakes.

The West Lancashire Light Railway's passenger stock, comprising an open-sided bogie toastrack, an enclosed bogie coach and a four-wheel brake van, seen at Hesketh Bank on 28 July 2002, while 0-4-0WT No.21 runs round. The building to the right is the engine shed.

eleven

The Ribble
Steam Railway

The Ribble Steam Railway, located at Preston Docks, has risen phoenix-like from the ashes of Steamport Southport which was based at the old Southport engine shed in Derby Road. In 1997 it was decided to move to a brown field site in Preston Docks and develop a new centre. With the proceeds from the sale of the Derby Road site new workshops, storage shed, museum and station have been constructed. The large and airy facilities are the envy of many more established railways. Passenger services began running in September 2005.

Much of the rolling stock from Steamport was brought to the Riverside centre and additional locomotives have joined the collection from the Fleetwood Locomotive Centre. The passenger trains run alongside the north bank of the River Ribble for 1 mile and cross the dock's marina on a swing bridge. The majority of the exhibits reflect the industrial history of the north-west of England. On site there are some forty industrial locomotives, representing no less than twenty different manufacturers, dating back as far as 1894, and as recently as the 1960s.

Heritage passenger trains and modern freight trains share the tracks at the centre where the fleet of preserved diesel shunters work incoming bulk bitumen trains. These are worked for Total Bitumen and have switched from road to rail since the Ribble Steam Railway re-located to Preston Docks. As one of the latest preserved railways to open to the public the Ribble Steam Railway seems well set on the road to success with superb restoration workshops and equally important modern, well-planned and clean public facilities.

The impressive new station and museum building seen on Saturday 17 June 2006 with Andrew Barclay 0-4-0ST (No.1147 of 1908) *John Howe* having just arrived with its two-coach train of BR Mark I coaches. In the background is the recently erected water tower from St Pancras station.

The Ribble Steam Railway has metamorphosed from Steamport Southport. Here on Sunday 8 June 1980 we see the ex-Mersey Railway 0-6-4T *Cecil Raikes* in the erstwhile engine shed at Southport. This tank engine is now in the custody of Liverpool Museums. The sale of this site helped finance the new facilities at Preston Docks.

Three of Steamport Southport's steam locomotives seen on 8 June 1980. Nearest the camera is *Cecil Raikes*, next is BR Standard Class '4MT' 2-6-0 No.76079 and furthest away is ex-GWR '5101' Class 2-6-2T No.5193. No.5193 is now on the West Somerset Railway where it has been converted to a 2-6-0 as No.9351.

Stanier 'Black Five' Class 4-6-0 No.44806 *Magpie* is also pictured inside the engine shed at Steamport on 8 June 1980. This locomotive is now based on the Llangollen Railway where it has had a lot of use. The Ribble Steam Railway's collection now concentrates on smaller industrial engines.

Andrew Barclay 0-4-0ST *Alexander* (No.1883 of 1922) has been restored as a museum exhibit alongside Ivatt Class '2MT' 2-6-0 No.46441 on loan from the Beet family and originally preserved at Steamtown Carnforth. *Alexander* carries a 'Steamport Limited' headboard as a reminder of the railway's origins.

The new workshops at the Preston Dock base make an interesting contrast with the old steam shed at Southport. The facilities here are second to none and must be the envy of most preserved railways. A number of boilers can be seen under restoration.

One of the more powerful diesel locomotives on the railway is this Swindon built ex-Western Region Class 14 diesel hydraulic 0-6-0, No.D9539. Entering service in 1965 No.D9539 spent most of its working life at the British Steel Corporation works at Corby. It arrived at Preston on 26 July 2005 from the Gloucestershire & Warwickshire Railway.

The beautifully restored Andrew Barclay 0-4-0ST (No.1147 of 1908) *John Howe* is pictured running round its train at the Ribble Steam Railway's Preston Docks terminus. In the siding behind the diminutive tank engine are some of the Total Bitumen wagons that are commercially worked over the dock railways by the RSR's diesel locomotives.

John Howe has run round its two-coach train and waits to take the day's third train out of the new station. The difference in size between the BR Mark I coaches and the small Andrew Barclay 0-4-0ST is very pronounced from this angle.

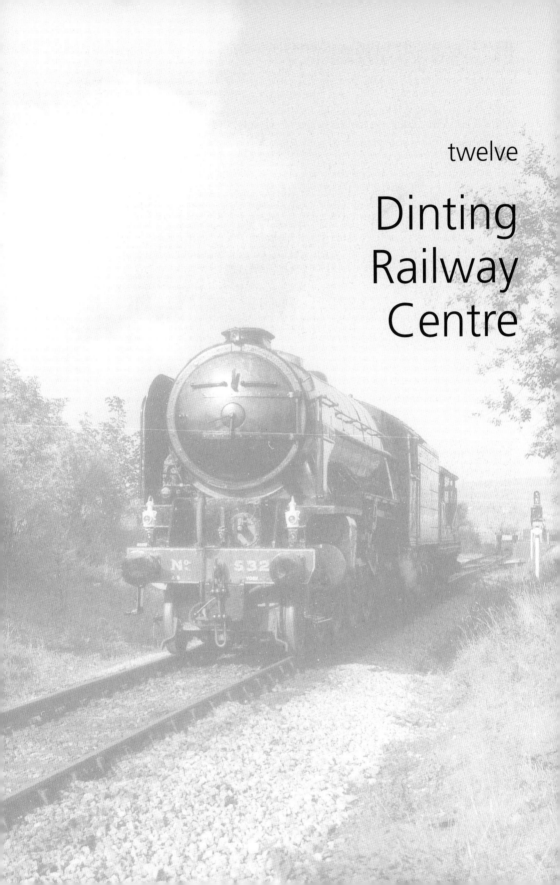

twelve

Dinting
Railway
Centre

Based on the small former Great Central Railway engine shed at Dinting, 2 miles on the Manchester side of Glossop in Derbyshire, the site was acquired by the 'Bahamas Locomotive Society' to house their Stanier 'Jubilee' Class 4-6-0 No.45596 *Bahamas*. The 10-acre site, leased from BR in August 1968, was derelict but the engine shed was renovated and an exhibition hall was built to provide covered accommodation for a growing number of locomotives. A demonstration line was laid to allow steam days to be held.

Apart from *Bahamas*, Dinting was home to an Austerity 0-6-0ST No.WD150 *Warrington*, re-built 'Royal Scot' Class 4-6-0 No.6115 *Scots Guardsman*, after it moved from the Keighley & Worth Valley at Haworth. The preserved LNWR 'Coal Tank' No.1054 also found a home at Dinting as did ex-CR Class '04' 2-8-0 No.63601, ex-Southern Railway 'Schools' Class 4-4-0 No.30925 *Cheltenham*, ex-LNER 'A4' Pacific No.60019 *Bittern* and 'A2' Pacific No.60532 *Blue Peter*. Eight industrial locomotives, ranging from *Southwick*, an 0-4-0 crane tank, to *Nunlow*, an 0-6-0T, were at one time or another based here. Other mainline locomotives to have visited Dinting in the course of working steam specials over the mainline included LMS 'Jubilee' Class 4-6-0 No.5690 Leander, LNER 'V2' 2-6-2 No.4771 *Green Arrow* and LNWR 2-4-0 No.790 *Hardwicke*.

In the late 1980s the society encountered difficulties over renewing their lease of the Dinting site. This ultimately brought about its closure with the society re-locating to Ingrow on the Keighley & Worth Valley Railway. In 1990 Ingrow goods shed was transformed into a workshop and museum as the 'Bahamas Locomotive Society' became an integrated part of the Worth Valley Railway. The 'Coal Tank' and No.45596 *Bahamas* became part of the operating fleet of the KWVR until withdrawn for overhaul. At the time of writing No.1054 is in the middle of a major overhaul.

The locomotive that brought about the creation of a railway centre at Dinting: Stanier 'Jubilee' or '5XP' Class 4-6-0 No.5596 *Bahamas*. Although in LMS livery, *Bahamas* was fitted with this ugly double chimney by British Railways and so should strictly speaking be in BR livery.

Single-chimney 'Jubilee' No.5690 *Leander* was based at Dinting during its first spell of mainline running and is seen with the LNWR 'Coal Tank' 0-6-2T No 1054 in the background. *Leander* is fitted with a single chimney which suits the elegant lines of the design so much better than *Bahamas'* ungainly double chimney.

The only Great Central Railway designed locomotive at Dinting was the Robinson '04' Class 2-8-0 No.63601 which is seen here framed by 0-6-2T No.1054 and the tender of *Cheltenham*. No.63601 was never restored while at Dinting; this had to wait until the 2-8-0 was transferred to the Great Central Railway based at Loughborough.

Maunsell 'Schools' Class 4-4-0 No.30925 *Cheltenham* was stored at Dinting and here is seen in the exhibition hall still carrying its final BR livery. *Cheltenham* was restored to Southern Railway livery for the 150th anniversary celebrations of the Rainhill Trials and is now displayed at the National Railway Museum in York.

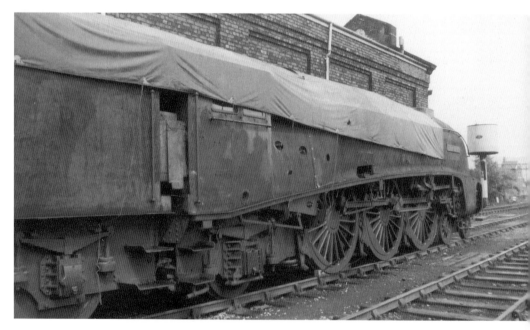

Despite being partially covered by a tarpaulin, Gresley 'A4' Pacific No.60019 *Bittern* is pictured stored alongside the single-road GCR engine shed at Dinting. *Bittern*, after spending some time masquerading as No.2509 *Silver Link*, is in the final throws of a major overhaul on the Mid Hants Railway which will see the 'A4' return to work on the mainline network.

thirteen

Other Railways and Steam Centres

A number of smaller preserved railways operate within Lancashire and Yorkshire and deserve to be included in this book.

The Abbey Light Railway

Founded in 1976 the narrow gauge Abbey Light Railway takes visitors to the eleventh-century Cistercian monastery of Kirkstall Abbey near Leeds. Operating on Sundays and Bank Holidays, the railway uses vintage internal combustion engines and rolling stock.

The Astley Green Colliery Museum

Located south of Astley Green Colliery near Tyldersley, Greater Manchester, this museum possesses a collection of over twenty colliery engines.

The Derwent Light Railway

The Derwent Light Railway is one of a small handful of railways that were not nationalised in 1948. Closed in the late 1980s, the line was mothballed until transformed into a cycleway. Half a mile of track was donated to the Yorkshire Farming Museum along with the necessary Light Railway Order allowing trains to operate between February and October.

The Elsecar Railway

Running between the Elsecar Heritage Centre, near Barnsley, to the canal basin at Hemingfield, this railway is laid on the Elsecar branch of the South Yorkshire Railway which opened in 1850. Trains run on Sundays from March to October.

Other titles published by Tempus

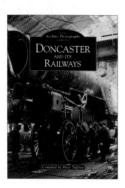

Doncaster and its Railways
PETER TUFFREY

This fascinating collection of over 200 photographs illustrates Doncaster's role in the history of the railways, from the early images of loco construction in the 1890s at the Doncaster Plant, through the glorious days of steam to diesels and electrics.

0 7524 0635 3

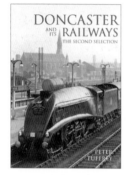

Doncaster and its Railways: The Second Selection
PETER TUFFREY

In this, his second book on Doncaster and its railways, Peter Tuffrey looks at the changing railway scene in and around Doncaster from the late nineteenth century to the present day. There are views of long-gone steam locomotives and modern diesels and electrics, as well as stations, the Plant and its employees, and coal, freight and passenger trains in and around Doncaster.

0 7524 2876 4

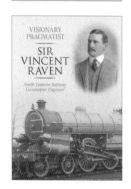

The Leek & Manifold Valley Light Railway
KEITH TURNER

The narrow gauge railways of Britain have some of the country's most beautiful scenery through which to run. The Leek & Manifold Valley Light Railway was no exception, running for 8 winding miles through the valleys of the rivers Manifold and Hamps. Situated in a corner of the Peak District National Park, this is the 'Manifold's' story from conception to closure and conversion to idyllic rural footpath.

0 7524 2791 1

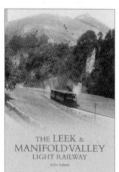

Sir Vincent Raven: North Eastern Railway Locomotive Engineer
ANDREW EVERETT

Raven's sole employer was the North Eastern Railway Co. He rose from engineering apprentice in 1875 to chief mechanical engineer from 1910. His steam locomotives were both stylish and practical. His advocacy of electric traction was visionary. Illustrated with archive photographs and ephemera, this biography explains Raven's career in the context of his life and times.

0 7524 3924 3

If you are interested in purchasing other books published by Tempus, or in case you have difficulty finding any Tempus books in your local bookshop, you can also place orders directly through our website
www.tempus-publishing.com